When I Saw Their Faces

Journey to Freedom

Henk Kaemingk

When I Saw Their Faces

All Scripture quotations, unless otherwise indicated, are taken from the New King James Version®. Copyright © 1982 by Thomas Nelson. Used by permission. All rights reserved.

Scripture quotations marked KJV are taken from the King James Version.

Cover picture, interior pictures, and map by Henk Kaemingk.

Copyright © 2017 Henk Kaemingk
All rights reserved.
ISBN-13: 978-90-826774-0-9
ISBN-10: 9082677407

BISAC Code: REL012120
BISAC Category: Religion / Christian Life / Spiritual Growth

Key words: Destiny, Sovereignty of God, True freedom, Purpose, Suffering.

henk.kaemingk@gmail.com

Available versions and editions:

English: When I Saw Their Faces
Paperback   ISBN 978-90-826774-0-9
E-book (Kindle version)   ISBN 978-90-826774-1-6
E-book (Epub version)   ISBN 978-90-826774-6-1

Dutch: Toen Ik Hun Gezichten Zag
Paperback   ISBN 978-90-826774-2-3
E-book (Kindle version)   ISBN 978-90-826774-3-0
E-book (Epub version)   ISBN 978-90-826774-7-8

Spanish: Cuando Vi Sus Rostros
Paperback   ISBN 978-90-826774-4-7
E-book (Kindle version)   ISBN 978-90-826774-5-4
E-book (Epub version)   ISBN 978-90-826774-8-5

Table of Contents

Acknowledgements vi

Preface vii

Introduction viii

Map x

My Childhood 1

   Journey to Canaan *1*

   The Dreams *7*

   Sold *11*

A Slave in Egypt 15

   The Darkness *15*

   The Light *22*

   Serving in Freedom *29*

   The Promotion *33*

The Prison 41

   Imprisoned *41*

The Battle *48*

The Victory *52*

Walking in Freedom *58*

The Officers *62*

The King's Court 73

The King's Dream *73*

The Ascent *82*

Ruler over Egypt *90*

Visitors from Canaan 97

Arrival of the Shepherds *97*

Benjamin *109*

Reunited *121*

The Reform 127

Management of the Provisions *127*

The Final Years *133*

Final Words 143

Notes and References 153

Acknowledgments

First, I thank God for the opportunity to express and share in written form what He has put in my heart through His Word and His Spirit.

I thank Edith—with whom He has allowed me to walk these past twenty-five years—for her encouragement to write this book and for her input, which has been essential to its present content. Together we have learned, and continue learning, the principles that form the foundation of this story.

I thank Carolina, Michael, Yoshiah, and Hezekiel for the vital and unique part that each has played in the realization of this book. I am grateful not only for their ideas and corrections to the text but, even more significantly, for the many conversations we have had about the topics discussed in this story—even long before the idea of writing a book was born.

Finally, I thank many others, including many of our students with whom we have had the privilege to share the Bible's teachings. They have, likely without knowing, contributed to the development of this story in different ways.

Preface

How relevant can a story—one that was written more than three thousand years ago—be to us who live in the twenty-first century? What can we learn? What can be of any use to us from a story about long-vanished people and cultures?

When we search a little bit deeper than the cultural context, we soon find that their greatest struggles and biggest questions were the same as ours: *Why do righteous people suffer? If God is both loving and almighty, why then is there suffering?* Questions such as these and many others have occupied the minds of humanity since the beginning of time and are as relevant today as they were then.

These are precisely the questions that are so prevalent in the Old Testament stories, and it is no doubt for that reason that they are preserved for us in so much detail. But does the fact that these stories *deal* with these questions mean that they also *answer* them? Maybe not on the surface. Just as gold is usually not found on the surface but only when we dig and search for it, once we start digging, we will soon discover that for those who search for these answers, there is no richer gold mine in the world than these ancient stories.

Introduction

I am glad you have decided to come and meet our host today! I can guarantee you that he will also be very happy to meet you and that he is more than willing to take the time to share his extraordinary story.

Allow me to start with a personal note. Very few lives have been as inspiring and encouraging to me as his. I listen to his story very often, and I try to apply the principles that I learn from him in my own life. However, I must admit that I still have a long way to go before I can say that I am truly living according to his example.

Before introducing you to him, I want to make a few comments that I think may be helpful to you. First of all, you will notice that when he talks about God, he often uses the name by which the Hebrew people know Him. In the text, this name is printed as *YHWH*. You may translate this for yourself in the way you prefer or are used to: for example, Lord, or Yahweh, or Jehovah. At other times, he calls Him *El Shaddai* or *Elohim*. Although to a great extent these three names are interchangeable, I have noticed that often he prefers using one over the others depending on the context or the attribute of God that he wants to emphasize. For example, when he wants to stress His power, he often likes to call Him *El Shaddai*, but when he is talking about his personal relationship with God or His specific purposes for his life, our host may prefer to use the name *YHWH*. When talking with Egyptians, he uses the

Egyptian word for God, which in this English text is translated as *God*.

You will also notice that our host sometimes repeats certain phrases. At first, it may seem to you that he has forgotten he said that already. But I can tell you with confidence that this is not the case. Rather, he does this with a purpose, often to draw a parallel with earlier events or to remind us of a similar situation that he shared before. Therefore, I invite you to pay special attention to those repetitions, which are usually an indication that he is dealing with the most relevant parts of his story.

Finally, I want to mention that in many places you will see small, raised numbers in the text. These numbers correspond to references at the end of the book. Some refer to verses taken from the chapters in Genesis where the Bible story about our host is found; they may serve to help us see which verses mention the particular parts or facts of his story. Others refer to verses from other Bible stories or teachings that deal with topics similar to the ones that he will share with us. The purpose of mentioning these references is to suggest studying or meditating on these Bible portions as a way to reach a deeper understanding of the spiritual meaning of the story and to enrich the application of it in our daily lives.

I have said enough now. I invite you to make yourself comfortable, and I wish you a wonderful visit with the man you have come to meet.

Henk Kaemingk

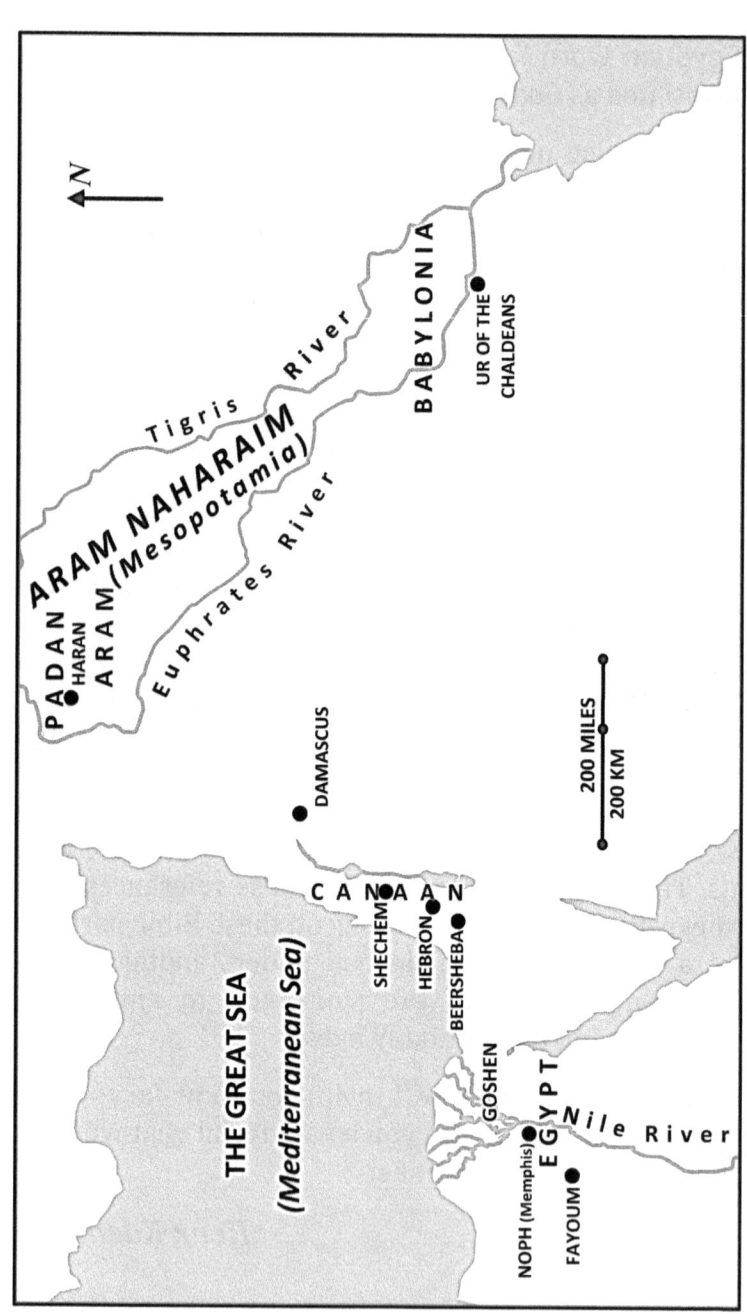

Chapter 1
My Childhood

Journey to Canaan

I must have been about six years old the day one of my father's servants came running to my mother and aunt. "You must come to the field immediately," he said. "Your husband wants to speak with you!"

When we arrived, I could see that my father was quite excited. He told us that Elohim had spoken to him through an angel in a dream. We had to leave my grandfather Laban's home in Padan Aram and return to the land where my father was born, the angel had told him. Father wanted us to get ready for the journey immediately. He was obviously happy with the angel's message. I knew that he had been having some problems and disagreements with my grandfather and uncles for a long time, and lately things had become even worse. My father had already talked about leaving a number of times, but even though my mother and aunt would always say that it was fine with them, that they would follow him wherever he wanted to go, he had never acted on his words.

Soon after the angel's announcement we were on our way to the land of Canaan. It was a very long journey.

Many things happened on the way; maybe we will have an opportunity to talk about that story some other time. Once in Canaan, my father chose Shechem as the place to get settled. After some time, however, we had trouble with the people there as well. So we had to pack up again. My father decided we should move farther south, to a place not far from Hebron where my other grandfather lived and where my father had grown up.

On the way, what I had thought would become the happiest day of my life in fact became a very sad one. It was the day my mother died, the same day my little brother was born. My father spent many days mourning. After he built a monument at the place where he had buried her, he said, "Now we must move on. Our pilgrimage has only just begun."

I will never forget the day I met my grandfather Isaac. He was blind and very old—very different from my grandfather in Padan Aram. His love for El Shaddai, the Almighty God, and his unconditional trust and faith in Him have always been a great inspiration and example to me. He thought every day could be his last day here on earth, and I could tell that he longed for El Shaddai to come and take him up to his "homeland," as he always called it.[1] Even though I admired—and in a sense envied—that attitude, I am still happy that El Shaddai left him here for many more years for me to enjoy and to learn from him.

So finally, we settled in the region of Hebron. During all the years of working for my grandfather in Padan Aram, my father had longed to be back in this land— the land he knew El Shaddai had chosen for him—to work for his own house.[2] However, the years that followed were not an easy or happy time for him, and therefore, neither were they for me. I loved my father very much, and it was difficult to watch how my brothers disrespected him.

In the beginning, I was not really aware of my brothers' attitudes and behavior. My father would send them out to take care of the flocks, and I always thought of them as responsible, hardworking sons. Later, I found out that even before we had arrived in Hebron, my three oldest brothers had already done things that hurt my father very much, and I doubt he had ever been able to forgive them completely.[3] When I grew up and joined my older brothers in the fields, I was shocked to discover their true character. I could hardly bear watching the things they did and hearing how they talked, especially about Father. When they realized I did not want to be a part of their actions and conversations, they warned me to not to tell Father anything I heard or saw. They would surely do something very bad to me the next time we went out, they threatened.

Out of fear, I decided to keep my mouth shut, but every time we came home and I saw my father's face, I could hardly deal with the unrighteousness done to him. I felt like such a coward and hypocrite—and even guilty of participating in my brothers' evil because I did not tell him the truth. For a time, I felt like I was being tossed back and forth like a wave by this double-minded attitude. Finally, I decided I had to be loyal to Father.

Grandfather had told me once that being deceived by your own son is the most painful thing that can happen to a father. I can still recall the expression I saw on his face when he spoke those words.

I knew that my brothers would hate me for betraying them and that many probably would call me a gossiper if I brought the report of their evil ways to my father. But I knew it was the will of El Shaddai for me to honor my father—that being obedient and loyal to him ought to be a higher priority to me than my own well-being and reputation. That conviction finally became the grounds for my decision. I became more and more open and honest with my father, bringing a report to him about everything that happened during our days out in the field.[4] As a result, he started trusting me more and more. In time, I realized that I was becoming his favorite child.

One day, when I came home from the field with my brothers, Father told me that he had something special for me. It was a long coat. When I put it on, it reached all the way to my feet.[5] It was a very special and beautiful coat, and I thought he had bought it from those merchantmen who used to travel the road through Canaan. They were actually relatives of ours, descendants of my grandfather's half brothers.[6] They traded between Egypt and Babylon, and on their way, they sometimes stopped to rest and greet my grandfather. They always brought news about our distant relatives and told us incredible stories about what they had seen in those great modern civilizations.

I was happy with the coat that my father had given me, but it also made me a little nervous. Do you know what such a special coat means in our culture? I tell you that only people in high positions use such coats. Therefore, as soon as I put it on, I understood that my father had chosen me as his heir and as the future chief and ruler of our tribe. This was not a complete surprise. No one in our family ever mentioned the topic, but I am sure that all of us actually already suspected Father had this idea in his mind. By giving me this coat, he now openly confirmed what all of us had thought for a long time.

I also knew that he had chosen me not just because of my special relationship with him as his favorite and beloved son. There is something else I have not told you yet.

My father had married two women, my aunt Leah and my mother, Rachel, and later he had also taken two concubines. In our culture, the heir would typically be the oldest son among the children of the wives. The sons of the concubines would never be the heirs. Therefore, my brother Reuben, the oldest son of my aunt Leah, really should have been the heir.

Now, one of the most hurtful things in our family was that my father did not love my aunt Leah. I believe that my grandfather in Padan Aram had somewhat forced my father to marry her. My father made no secret of the fact that he did not love her. Once he said to all my brothers, "You know that my wife bore me two sons," referring to my little brother and me.[7] With that, he clearly rejected my aunt as his wife and assigned her the position of concubine. I know that my father was wrong in rejecting her and her sons, and I have always believed that his attitude toward them contributed to their lack of respect for him.

So when my father gave me the coat, it was more than a nice gift for a spoiled child. It was a public declaration that my mother was his only wife, and therefore, I, her oldest son, was his heir. You can imagine that every time my brothers saw the coat, it just reminded them of being rejected, fueling their anger and jealousy toward me.

At the time, I did not understand it as clearly as I do now. I think that the way I used that coat in front of them showed a lack of wisdom, to say the least. You see, in many ways, my family is unique, but in some ways, it is also like any other family—not one of us is totally right, and probably nobody is completely wrong either.

Nonetheless, when I think back on those times when I was a boy, when I try to dig deep into my heart to honestly discern my own motives, I believe that in my attitude toward my father—in telling him about the bad behavior of my brothers—I was not just gossiping or trying to secure my position as the favorite child and heir. I honestly believe that I was driven by true indignation about the unrighteousness toward my father, by a sincere desire to be a loyal son to him. What do you think? Could my heart be deceiving me?

"Search me, O Elohim, and know my heart: try me, and know my thoughts, and see if there be any wicked way in me," I prayed, acknowledging and confessing that it was impossible for me to be completely sure about what the deepest motivation of my own heart was.[8] Only Elohim would know this; only Elohim could reveal it. And He did, though it took a very long and painful road.

On the one hand, I wish nobody the suffering this journey caused, but on the other hand, I would not trade this experience for all the gold in the world. Walking this road has made me the man I am today, the man I needed to become in order to fulfill the calling and reach the destiny that Elohim had for me and that He would soon start to reveal.

The Dreams

One morning, I woke up and thought, "What in the world does this mean?" I had just had an extremely weird dream.

You might say, "So what? We all get weird dreams every now and then." I know, but this dream was different. I cannot explain why, but I just knew that this was a message—a revelation from Elohim. In my dream, I saw my brothers and myself working in the field. We were all binding sheaves. Suddenly, my sheaf stood straight up. Next, the sheaves of my brothers stood up around mine and bowed down before it. "Why," you will ask me, "did you think this was such a special dream?"

Well, as I thought about it, it seemed to me that Elohim could be showing me He indeed wanted me to be my father's heir and become the prince and ruler of our people! "What shall I do with this revelation? Shall I keep it to myself?" I thought. "No, this is a word from Elohim. This is not just for me; it affects all of us. When I tell my brothers, they will surely change their attitude toward me. They will meditate on the meaning of the dream and at least consider that Elohim could be confirming my father's decision to choose me as the heir. They cannot possibly ascribe this message to my own pride or desires! Only Elohim can send dreams; nobody can make up or even manipulate their own."

I completely misjudged what my brothers' reactions would be. They were furious! "Do you really think that you will rule and reign over us?" they scolded.

I never said that! I did not say a word about the meaning of the dream. I only told them what I had seen. *They* were the ones who said it represented me ruling over them. Were they right? At the time, I secretly thought they probably were. But seeing how it all has unfolded, I actually have a different thought about it. Whatever the real meaning was, after all this, they hated me even more than before. Maybe you will say that it was unwise of me to tell them the dream, and now, looking back, I think you are probably right. I can see that I lacked wisdom, as many seventeen-year-old boys do.

If the dream I just mentioned made such an impression on me, imagine what the next dream did to me. I saw myself standing, and suddenly the sun, the moon, and eleven stars came and bowed down before me! When I woke up, I felt excited but afraid at the same time. I really had no doubt that this again was a message from Elohim—another revelation from Him about His plan for my life. That whole day, I meditated on what I should do next.

"If I share this with my brothers, they will get even angrier," I thought. "Or maybe not…when they hear that I had similar dreams twice, might they consider that it most likely did come from Elohim after all?"

I wanted to be wiser this time though. I would not tell just my brothers, as I had with the first dream. "I will tell Father. He will understand! He will even be happy to learn that Elohim is confirming his belief that I should become a ruler," I thought. "He will surely want to use this as an opportunity to convince my brothers that it is, in fact, the design of Elohim that I become a chief."

I also expected my brothers to be more indifferent and to care less about this second dream—or at least to not feel offended by it. After all, the main reason why they had been so mad about the first dream was the role that they had played in the dream. They were the ones represented by the sheaves bowing down to me. They did not mainly oppose the thought of me becoming a ruler so much as the idea that *they* would be the ones under my rule. This second dream had some obvious similarities, but it was also significantly different—especially because my brothers were not in the dream. I had only seen the sun, the moon, the stars, and myself. It did not necessarily concern them.

After thinking long and hard, I made up my mind and decided to take the risk and share the dream. That evening, when Father and all of us were together, I told them what I had seen. When I finished, I felt my heart pounding in my chest and did not dare to look up. How would they react? I felt great relief when Father started responding before my brothers could speak a word. But almost immediately, this relief turned into great disappointment when I realized that, instead of supporting me—supporting his own case, for that matter—he rebuked me!

"What kind of dream is that?" he said. "Do you think that your mother and I, and your brothers, will come and bow down before you?"

I never said that! I had said, "The sun, the moon, and eleven stars..." I did not say—I did not *know*—whom they represented. It was my father's interpretation that these represented him, my mother, and my brothers.

Was he right? At the time, I honestly thought he could be, mainly because of the coincidence in the number of stars. However, my mother had already died, so I knew that this explanation of the dream could not be completely accurate. Looking back now, I can see other possible interpretations, but of course, I did not know then all that I know now.

I hope you can see my reasons for sharing the second dream, even after the bad experience with the first one. Was it right? Was it wise? Was it wrong or unwise? I am not so sure. What I do recognize now is that I was probably trying to "help" Elohim to convince my brothers. That was not what Elohim had intended for me to do with the dreams. If He had wanted to convince my brothers, He could have given the dreams to them instead of me.

I have learned that receiving a dream, vision, or prophecy is a great responsibility. We need a lot of wisdom from Elohim to know with whom to share them, when to share them, and even if we are to share them at all. In the same way, we need clear direction from Elohim to know how to act on them, when to act on them, and even if we are to act on them at all. Maybe you will say, "If we are not to act on it, why would Elohim give us the dream, vision, or prophecy then?" I will share later what I learned about that, but let me first finish the story of my childhood.

Sold

Well, my childhood ended very abruptly. It happened at a time when my ten older brothers had gone way north with the flocks, to Shechem, where my father's property was—the property we had abandoned years before. They would sometimes remain in that area for many days. One day, when they had been gone for quite some time, my father asked me to go and see how they were doing. I put on my long coat and started the trip. After asking around for a while, I found them. The way they looked at me and whispered to one another when I came closer made me feel very uncomfortable. I could tell that they were up to something. All of a sudden, they jumped up and grabbed me, took my coat off, and dragged me to a pit, where they threw me in. It was an empty pit; there was no water in it. They scolded me from above. "Hey, dreamer, do not make any illusions for yourself about Father's inheritance. You will surely die in this pit!"

Many thoughts raced through my mind. Would they really be so cruel as to let me die in this pit? That could not be. I knew that they were capable of severe cruelty—a few of them had already killed many people—but surely they must draw the line somewhere.[9] I knew they hated me, but I was still their brother! And even if they did not care about me, they must have had some respect left for Father; he would be totally devastated if I did not come home, and they knew that. I did not know what to think or what to do. Should I cry for help? No one could hear me except my brothers. Would my crying soften their hearts? Or would the signs of my despair only give them more pleasure?

What a relief I felt when, after a few hours, they threw down a rope to pull me up! I thought that it had all just been a bad joke to scare me. When I came out, I saw that some of my brothers were talking with a group of those traveling merchants. I noticed they took some money from them, and I wondered what kind of trick they were playing this time. Would they be selling some of my father's sheep?

Then, the unbelievable happened. As they tied my hands together and pulled me with a rope to where the merchants' camels were standing, I realized that they had sold me as a slave! When the camels started walking, I cried out to my brothers, still hoping that one of them—maybe Reuben, who was always a little more softhearted toward me than the others—would show mercy and save me.

It was in vain. I finally stopped crying when we were so far away that I knew they could not hear me anymore. When we came closer to the area of Hebron, I had some hope in me that something miraculous would happen, but once we passed Beersheba, I was left with only desperation.

My Childhood

I felt completely helpless, without hope, as I was forced to travel the long road through the desert that followed. I knew that we were heading for Egypt, and from their conversations, I understood that the merchants were planning to sell me there. They gave me enough food and water during the trip, but obviously only because they wanted me to be in good enough condition to make some profit on me. I knew that I had no chance of escaping, and even if I had managed to get loose from the ropes with which I was bound, I would surely not have survived the way back to Canaan. I do not remember how long the road was in reality—maybe twelve days or two weeks—but it seemed like an eternity to me.

When we arrived in Egypt, I did not know whether to feel relieved or not. I knew that the long and painful journey was finally over, but I also feared that what was coming next would be even longer and more painful. They took me to a marketplace, where I was sold to an important-looking man. Two other men, apparently slaves of his, took me to his homestead. They immediately put me to work there with other slaves of low rank, who looked at me as if I were a strange creature. I knew that they talked about me among themselves, but I could not understand anything of their Egyptian tongue.

This whole journey through the desert, my coming to the land of Egypt and being sold to this Egyptian man—it all seemed so unreal to me. All this time, I had kept thinking that it could not be true—hoping that I would wake up soon from this terrible dream to find out that I was just in my father's tent in Hebron. Of course, that did not happen. When I lay down that first night in my new "home," I finally accepted these things: it is real, it is true, and I will never see my father again. I am a slave in Egypt.

Chapter 2
A Slave in Egypt

The Darkness

The man who had bought me from the merchants was named Potiphar. In the beginning, I had no clue what was going on here or what this place was all about; I just did the jobs they showed me to do. After some time, though, when I started understanding the language and talking with the other slaves, I realized that my new master was actually a very important man in the country. He was the chief of security for the king. He was a very strict and demanding—yet righteous—man. He had a busy life and was away from home often.

He had many slaves who worked in his house as well as in his fields. Some of the slaves had high positions; they served as stewards over different areas of his homestead. I understood that they were usually the older slaves, although at the time, it was hard for me to estimate their ages. They all looked very young to me because they did not have hair or beards. Others, evidently usually the younger ones, stood under the stewards and had more specific responsibilities and simple jobs.

I was, of course, among the lowest, and you could say that my jobs usually were the ones considered the very lowest. I felt that everybody looked down on me, not only because I was the youngest and lowest of all, but also—or mainly, I should probably say—because I was not an Egyptian. Little by little, as I started understanding their conversations, I realized how proud they all were of being Egyptian. They were not joking; they really believed they were superior to everybody else in the world, even though they were slaves just as I was.

What hurt me even more than the fact that I was looked down upon and separated from my family was the suffering I knew my father was going through. How hard must his grief have been, having lost me, worrying about not knowing where I was! What would my brothers have told him? I was sure that they had not told him the truth; they were always very good at making up stories to cover up their actions and explain things that had gone wrong. Oh, how could they be so hardened that they would not care, seeing my father suffering and mourning, and simply say that they did not know what had happened to me?

My greatest pain, however, came from the confusion about where Elohim was in all this. I had no doubt that the dreams I had had were from Him. But if Elohim had showed me so clearly that His plan for my life was that I become my father's heir and the ruler of his descendants, how then could all this be happening to me? Was He not El Shaddai, the all-powerful, eternal Creator of all things?

"How can it be that He says one thing and does another thing, contrary to His word?" I thought. "How can it be that He designs one thing, but another thing actually happens, contrary to His design? Where is His wisdom, and where is His power to work all things according to that wisdom?"

In that time of confusion, I started meditating on what I really believed about *YHWH*, whom we in our family sometimes called "the Elohim of the heavens."[1] I started remembering and meditating on my father's stories about the times when *YHWH* had appeared and spoken to him—especially my favorite one, when He had called Himself "*YHWH* the Elohim of your father, Abraham, and the Elohim of Isaac."[2] Every time I heard that, or even just remembered it, I would feel chills all over my body from the profound impact of those words and my deep respect for His name. Also, my grandfather had often told me about the times when *YHWH* had appeared to him and that He had called Himself "the Elohim of your father Abraham."[3]

For as long as I can remember, I have always believed in *YHWH* as being El Shaddai, the Almighty Elohim, Creator of all things, the only true God. My grandfather in Padan Aram had some *teraphim* that he called "my gods."[4] I never really understood that, but at the time, as a little boy, I did not think much about it either. I know that my mother gave them some importance; she brought a few with her when we moved.[5] But once we arrived in Canaan, my father told her to get rid of them.[6]

The people among whom we lived in Canaan had many gods, but in our family, we were always very strict to worship and believe in only *YHWH*. Our strong devotion to *YHWH* and our strict separation from all other gods has a long history and very deep roots. It goes back to the time when my great-grandfather still lived in the land of the Chaldeans. It was there where *YHWH* appeared to him for the first time. That was when He told him to leave the land of his fathers and when for the first time He spoke to him the promise that we in our family call *the Blessing of Abraham*, or sometimes just *the Blessing*.[7]

Before continuing my story, I must first explain to you what this promise, this Blessing, means to us. For you to understand my story, you must understand that to us, in our family, nothing is more holy—nothing is of higher value—than the Blessing. This is what gives us our identity as a family. It constitutes the very purpose of our existence, the foundation of our faith, and the reason to believe in the things we hope for without ever having seen them. Because of the Blessing, we know that *YHWH* has special promises for us.

Later on in my great-grandfather's life, not long before my grandfather was born, *YHWH* appeared again to him and helped him understand that the Blessing made him and his descendants, who would be the heirs of the Blessing, a special people—a chosen people, separate and different from all others. This is also the reason why we are all circumcised. The circumcision signifies that we are set apart from all other people, and it reminds and warns us to not to mix with them in any way.[8]

After my great-grandfather died, *YHWH* appeared to my grandfather and made him the heir of the Blessing.[9]

My grandfather loved to tell me that story over and over again, and I never got tired of hearing it over and over again. He would always conclude with, "And therefore we know that we are His own people. *YHWH* has chosen us for Himself, to become a great nation, and one day He will give us this land to be our own," referring to the land where we dwelled, which today is still possessed by the Canaanite people.

I also know that *YHWH* has chosen my father to inherit the Blessing from his father and that He will confirm it to us, my father's descendants, from generation to generation as an everlasting covenant.[10] You can imagine that it was very special for me to consider us as a people different from all others, chosen by El Shaddai Himself—holy, separated, and set apart. Many times, I even felt proud of being part of such an elect and elite group, to realize that Elohim had preferred us above all other nations. I always sensed that I was part of something very special and exclusive, especially during the times when I sat down listening to my grandfather as he spoke concerning the things to come, things he knew and believed based on the promises that were contained in the Blessing.

And now, here I was—in Egypt. A huge confusion came over me. I felt as if I was lost in the midst of a dense darkness. What should I believe about *YHWH*, about His will, His promises, His power? This confusion became greater and greater as I meditated on the contrast between the things I had hoped for and believed in and the reality that was now in control of my life. At times, this filled me with indignation and anger because of the strong belief that everything that was happening to me was wrong in the eyes of *YHWH*, not in accordance with His will and design.

The Blessing, the promises, the testimonies of my fathers, my heritage, my dreams—they had all come from Him. I knew it.

"Therefore, it cannot be right that I am now here," I thought. "I must be with my family. I must be part of the fulfillment of the will and purposes of my Elohim. I cannot allow myself to become mixed in with these people here. With all my heart, soul, and strength, I must resist becoming integrated with a nation that is not His. Does not the fact that *we* are the chosen imply that *they* are the rejected? How can it be right that I am now part of this people? Was I not born and called to be separate? How can it be right that I dedicate my life and strength to those who are not His chosen people? Surely it cannot be the will of Elohim that I am here and that this uncircumcised Egyptian keeps me from fulfilling His will and plan for my life! I must do something. I must resist, rebel, try to escape and to return to Canaan!"

At other times, however, my doubts would sweep me to the other extreme. "Can it be that anything happens against the will of El Shaddai, the Almighty One? Is He not sovereign over all circumstances? If this is indeed against His will, how then can this actually be happening? Must I consider, then, that this possibly is the design of Elohim—that He for some unfathomable reason wants it to be this way? In that case, would my rebellion against Potiphar then be rebellion against Him?"

If only I had had an answer! What would my great-grandfather have done? What would my grandfather have done? Oh, I wished that *YHWH* appeared to me as He had to my fathers. But He never did. He did not even give me another dream.

It was in this time of double-mindedness that I called on and cried out to *YHWH*. I decided to believe that He would hear me. "I know that You can see me and hear me. Answer me and guide me, as You have guided my forefathers in times of doubt and confusion, I pray. Even though I neither see You nor hear You, I know that You are here. You are the One who lives and sees me." (That is what my great-aunt had once said, and it has become one of the favorite phrases in our family.[11])

During that time, I was learning to work with horses and mules here. In Padan Aram and in Canaan, it was well known that the Egyptians had many horses, but we only knew camels and donkeys. We did not know horses; most of us had hardly ever seen one. It struck me now how these animals must be dominated with bits and bridles. "Why are they so stubborn?" I thought. "Why are they resisting? Once I teach them what to do, why do they not just kneel down like a camel and serve their master?"

As I reflected on their behavior, a mysterious and disconcerting feeling came over me. Could I, through my resistance, be similar to them? That was a terrible and convicting idea, but I could not erase it from my mind. And sometimes when I observed their rebellious and obstinate attitude, it seemed like I was looking in a mirror.

"I do not want to be like them. Am I resisting You? Are You trying to teach me, but I refuse to kneel down for You? Are you trying to lead me, but I am resisting following You? I acknowledge my rebellion, O *YHWH*! I want to be faithful to You, I want to come near to You and enter into Your presence. *I do not want to be like a horse or a mule, which does not come near to you unless controlled by bit and bridle. Teach me, guide me, lead me, instruct me, and show me the way in which I should go.*"[12]

The Light

One night, I lay awake for many hours. I could hear the sound of all the other slaves sleeping. Suddenly a bright light came on. No, not a literal light, but a thought that sprang up in my mind, and it shook me up. "Do you really know what the substance of the Blessing is? Do you remember the words that I have spoken to your fathers?" I knew that it was *YHWH* speaking to me. As I meditated on the questions He was asking me, the words of the Blessing echoed in my head:

"I will make you a great nation; I will bless you and make your name great. And you shall be a blessing...and in you all the families of the earth shall be blessed."[13]

And you will be a blessing! That was it! All of a sudden I saw it as clear as a lamp shining before me. Suddenly, I understood that the very essence, the very purpose of the Blessing was that we, the people of *YHWH*, the chosen, were to be a blessing to all other nations! How could I have missed this? How could I have thought for so many years that we were chosen to be the only ones that Elohim wanted for Himself? Suddenly I could clearly see that *YHWH* loves all other nations just as much as He loves us and that He had chosen us to be a vessel, an instrument in His hand, to use us for the purpose of blessing them all! How could I have been so wrong? How could I have believed that *YHWH* would be so exclusive as to choose only us for Himself and to reject all others? How could I have believed that there is partiality, favoritism with Elohim?[14]

Now I could see what the Blessing really meant. No, the fact that we are the chosen does *not* imply the rejection of the other nations. On the contrary, the Blessing of Abraham is the way by which Elohim means to reach, to bless, and to include all nations! Is *YHWH* the Elohim of Abraham, Isaac, and Jacob only? Is He not also the Elohim of the nations? Yes, of the nations also![15] What a revelation!

Well, I admit that this truth was never hidden, but I had been so blind that I had not seen it. Now that I saw it, I could not understand anymore how I could have ever missed it!

I started feeling embarrassed, even hating myself for having had those attitudes of pride and superiority. I thought about the way many Egyptians had made me feel with their similar attitude toward me, and I reflected on how we must have made others feel when we had displayed these attitudes. How was it possible that I, considering myself as one of the chosen, had shown the exact same attitude that I abhorred in those whom I considered the rejected?

That night, I bowed down before *YHWH* and repented in dust and ashes. "Forgive me, my Elohim, for having been so blind, so foolish, and so stubborn. I will no longer be as a horse or a mule; I will be humble like the foal of a donkey. Teach me, guide me, lead me, and instruct me. Show me the way in which I should go."

The more I meditated on this completely new approach and even new interpretation of the Blessing, the more I repented. I continued finding more and more attitudes in my heart that I needed to repent of and ask *YHWH*'s forgiveness for. I started reflecting not only on what my response to Potiphar and the people in Egypt should be now, but also on how our attitude toward the Canaanites had always been. My grandfather had often told me that we should bless them, and I knew that earlier in his life, he had been a very well-respected man among them.[16] But I had never really understood his reasoning. I had been afraid to question or contradict him, though, so I just never responded to those words. Our opinion at home was different, however.

"These Canaanites are not the people of *YHWH*. He has prepared them for destruction. Elohim will destroy them and give us their land." And that opinion was often reflected in our attitude toward them.

As I now meditated on that, I saw the righteousness and wisdom of my grandfather. I felt a heavy burden for not having understood—much less fulfilled—our calling. Had we ever realized what a responsibility it was to be the chosen? The Canaanites knew that we were the people of *YHWH*—they even called us that! But they also knew very well how we lived, how we treated one another, and how we treated them. Just thinking of that made me feel so ashamed and so guilty of profaning the name of *YHWH* among these nations.[17] How could it be that we had always felt so special about being *the chosen*, and yet, at the same time, we had been so superficial, had lacked seriousness about what it really meant?

The more I meditated, the more I could see my selfishness and pride. Had we not arranged the whole issue in such a way that it had become all about us instead of about *YHWH*? Had it not all become about what He had for us—the promises, the land, the great nation, and all that? Had we ever thought about what His purpose in all this was—what He expected from us, instead of what we thought to expect from Him? If we were really a separate people, a different people, why then were our lives so much the same as all others? Why did we seek the same things the other nations sought, using the promises as the means to find and obtain them? If Elohim had such special purposes for us, then how come we had aspired to the same purposes as all others?[18] How could we have fallen down in such a deep pit, so bound by slavery to our own pride, dreams, and ambitions?

"Tonight, I give it all up. From now on, it is no longer about me or about my dreams or about what You have promised me. From now on, it is about You. From now on, You are my Master. I need You to pull me up from this pit and liberate me from my slavery. Only You can set me free." That night, I felt that I had found true freedom. Now that my eyes were opened and I had seen the light, I could see that the only way to be truly free was by serving *YHWH* and living for His purposes—by being His faithful slave!

Finding and understanding my true freedom did not mean that, from that day on, all my struggles and sufferings were over. It helped me put everything into perspective in my mind, but my emotions were still far behind, far from being satisfied or under control. I still suffered the grief of being ripped away from my father's house, and I still felt the pain when I imagined my father's grieving. On top of that, I started worrying about my little brother. How would he be doing? My brothers had never cared much about his very existence, but what would that be like when he started growing up? I had no doubt that he was now my father's favorite, and I could easily imagine my brothers turning their hatred on him, now that they had gotten rid of me.

Many times, my emotions not only refused to come under the control of the truth that Elohim had revealed to me, but even tried to bring me back under *their* control. I realized that there were many more battles to be fought so that I might live in victory and dwell in this new freedom. The war was far from over. There were times when my emotions managed to obscure the reality of the truth of *YHWH*; they challenged me with questions about the evidence of His power and His sovereignty and of the fulfillment of His promises. They tried to bring me back into the slavery of my dreams. But I started fighting back. "I have a new Master now; I will no longer listen to you," I would bravely and firmly reply.

The fact that I now understood what my real freedom was did not mean that I was capable of seeing and understanding the purpose of all that had happened, all I was going through. However, strangely enough, that was not as relevant anymore. I mean, although I still desired and even tried to understand the purpose, I did not *need* to understand it all in order to have peace and even joy. It was not the understanding of my circumstances but the understanding of the sovereignty of El Shaddai *over* them that was my source of peace and joy. I discovered that it was not necessary to understand my circumstances; what I needed to understand was how to respond to them.

What helped me greatly in this was remembering the stories of the battles my forefathers had gone through. They had told me about times of not understanding *YHWH*, like the story of my great-grandfather's obedience when *YHWH* called him, when he went out, not knowing where he was going.[19] Those were the times when they had learned to persevere through believing and trusting Him.

I remembered the many occasions when Elohim had led my fathers through valleys of the shadow of death. In those times, they had learned to trust Him—to fear not, believing that He was always with them, even when they did not see His promises being fulfilled and when they could not understand His ways. I had never liked those stories so much; I had always preferred the more victorious ones, like the glorious appearances of *YHWH*, or the stories about great prosperity, like the exceeding increase of their stock and the extraordinary harvest of crops.[20]

But now I started appreciating the stories about their afflictions! I began to understand that anyone will count it all joy when the presence of *YHWH* is almost visible and tangible through the favors bestowed upon them. However, would it not be of much higher virtue and excellence if I could recognize His presence, and even experience the *joy* of His presence, in the midst of trials and tribulation—not seeking deliverance according to my own desires and understanding but accepting in faith that His ways and thoughts are always higher than mine?[21] That would surely be peace and joy that surpasses human understanding![22] Foolishness, surely, in the eyes of man, but in truth, it is the power of El Shaddai, who lifts us above our own desires to help us walk in a disposition to be used by Him for the fulfillment of His eternal purposes.

My battles continued for many months, not only to bring every thought of my understanding into captivity to the obedience to Elohim, but also to submit my feelings and emotions to the governing of truth.[23] As I gradually progressed in victory, the world became different to me. I knew that *YHWH* was with me. I had felt His presence many times before, ever since I was a little child, but now it was different. Now I knew that I *dwelt* in His presence; no longer did I depend on what I felt. Nor did His presence come and go. I realized that He was teaching me and guiding me. I understood that He was leading me, even when I did not understand many facts and details of my circumstances.

Serving in Freedom

The fundamental truth that Elohim was showing me was that He had chosen me to be a blessing, wherever I was and to anyone He brought into my life. That truth was like a bright star on the horizon that travelers in the desert would point to as a fixed marker that directed every step, allowing them to travel securely without getting lost, even in the dark. Even when my understanding and emotions were in darkness, the one thing that I always understood was that it was the will of Elohim for me to be a blessing, here and now. That understanding became a lamp before my feet that showed me how to walk, how to obey, how to respond, how to speak, when to remain silent, and how to act in every situation.

YHWH had chosen me to be a blessing...to Potiphar. I had now come to understand that it was the will of El Shaddai for me to honor Potiphar, and that being obedient and loyal to him ought to be my highest priority. Being a blessing to Potiphar—honoring and obeying him and serving him as best as I could—would be my way of honoring, obeying, and pleasing *YHWH*. And even more than that. I also came to the conviction that He wanted me to be a blessing to everyone else around me—the stewards and all my fellow slaves here at the master's homestead.

This is our call, purpose, and destiny as the chosen people of *YHWH*, to be a blessing to everyone everywhere—not to feel superior, but in lowliness of mind, esteem all others better than ourselves. So, with the help of El Shaddai, I decided to become more than an obedient slave; I wanted to truly honor my master and be loyal, faithful, and trustworthy, even in the very little things. I chose to serve him as a king—not according to what he deserved, but according to what El Shaddai, my true Master, deserved.[24]

As I walked in this newness of heart and mind, by the grace of El Shaddai, miracles started to happen. Miraculously, I started loving my master! It began to bother me watching the things some other slaves did when he was gone and listening to the way they sometimes talked about him. They all obeyed him, of course, but even some of the older and higher slaves manifested attitudes of disrespect and disloyalty during his absence. Then, when he was present, they talked and acted with hypocrisy as if they were humble and faithful servants. I sometimes wondered how much he was aware of that situation, of the way these slaves acted behind his back. Often, when I saw his face, I felt sorry for him, and sometimes I desired to tell him. I was afraid to do so, though; I knew that the other slaves would get very mad at me. "And, well," I tried to justify myself, "the master will not believe me anyway." But this excuse could never liberate me completely from feeling like a coward.

Somehow, the master must have discerned the different attitude that Elohim had put in my heart. For some reason, it seemed that I started to draw his attention. Sometimes he talked with me, which surprised me. He was a very busy man, and I really never saw him taking time to chat with his lower slaves. Once he asked me about my childhood—where I came from. I could see his eyes wander off as I told him my story, and I wondered what he was thinking.

One day, he asked me what I, a son of a very wealthy shepherd, thought of being a slave in Egypt. I had already noticed that the people here did not have a very high opinion of shepherds, but knowing that my father owned very large herds made him recognize that he was indeed a man worthy of respect.[25] At first, I did not know how to answer; I was afraid of saying something that would be offensive. Then I said that I was a worshipper of *YHWH*, the living and true God, Creator of all things.[26] I told him that I believed that *YHWH* had brought me here. "He is El Shaddai, the Almighty One," I said. "I believe that there is nothing that can happen without His permission and that He is powerful to give purpose to everything that happens, for the fulfillment of His plans."

I continued explaining that I knew *YHWH* was with me, even if things were hard or seemed unjust, and that *YHWH* was the One who gave me strength to endure the hardships. He stood there just listening to me, staring at the ground. Then he looked me in the eyes, and without saying a word, he walked away. I could tell that he was meditating on what I had said. I deeply desired that my testimony would help him see the contrast between the Living God and the Egyptian gods.

"You are our Elohim, the Elohim of the children of Abraham—not in the sense of being *exclusively* ours, but in the sense of being revealed by us, through us, and in us. You have chosen us for the task of making You known among the nations. That is our mission and our calling."

I realized that I was finding favor in the eyes of Potiphar. My taskmaster began to charge me with jobs that were more meaningful and involved more responsibility. I had no doubt that Potiphar himself had commanded him to do so. Sometimes the master himself would even come out to give me orders personally, or he would give me a compliment on a job that I had done. I will never forget the day when he asked me to do a particularly challenging job, a job much beyond my normal duties and expertise. Later, I reported to him that I was finished, and when he inspected my work, I could tell from his face that he was surprised and pleased. Then he looked at me and said, "You are right—I can see that *YHWH* is with you." His approval of me and my job was a great encouragement, but what meant even more to me was that he had used the name of *YHWH*![27]

Many of the slaves started noticing this special attention, especially when my responsibilities included overseeing jobs that other slaves were working on. It was quite humiliating for the Egyptian slaves to be supervised by a *Hebrew*, as they called me. Many people called us "the Hebrews," also in Canaan. In itself, that was not at all an offensive or despicable name. However, here in Egypt, it could sound like that—not really because they thought lowly of Hebrews, but more because they thought so highly of themselves.

The comments the slaves made about the master's attitude toward me were just funny jokes at first, but as time went on, they started reflecting some jealousy. I tried to pay no attention to that and just do my work. When they made comments directly to me, I would simply ignore them and pretend that I had not heard or understood anything. Later, however, I detected some meanness in their words, and sometimes I started fearing aggression from them. As my responsibilities slowly but continually kept increasing, so did the significance of my position and the relevance of my presence in the master's household. My master trusted me more and more, and I realized that, little by little, I was becoming his favorite slave. At the same time, the other slaves started envying me more and more, and sometimes I felt that they looked at me as if I were wearing a long coat!

The Promotion

One day, the master came home and told me that he needed to talk with me immediately. He looked very serious, and I could not discern if he was angry or at peace with me. He took me into his house, together with the stewards. He said that he had decided to make some adjustments and that the main change was that I would become the first steward, the overseer of all he had—in the house as well as in the field, his entire homestead. I could not believe my ears. I felt honored, as you might imagine...but it also made me very nervous. Just try to imagine what it would mean to all the Egyptian slaves to receive orders from or to be corrected by a Hebrew steward!

For some time, I had already had a few of the lower and younger slaves under my supervision. But now, also even the older slaves—the stewards who for many years had managed the estate during the master's frequent absences—would come under my authority. I knew for sure that I would be confronted with feelings of jealousy and at times maybe even anger from them. If the master had asked me to accept this new position, I do not know what I would have answered. But he did not ask—that was not his style. He just told us that he had decided to establish this new order. None of the stewards said anything, but the environment was very tense. Then he told me that I could go and that he would talk with me later. The stewards remained with him (the *other* stewards, I should say now). I had a feeling that some very heavy issues were going to be discussed among them.

A short time later, he called me and talked with me alone. I dared to tell him that I really appreciated his trust in me but that I thought it too high a responsibility for me to accept this position. "I have never been in a position of authority, except for the few lower slaves here in your household; I really do not know how to give orders and such."

"Are you resisting me?" he asked.

"No, but I feel that I cannot be in authority here. I do not have the preparation or the capacity to give orders."

"Let me explain something to you. You know that I give many orders, not only in my house, but anywhere in Egypt, as the chief of security in this country. Have you observed how everyone obeys me? Do you know why? That is because I obey the orders of Pharaoh. The foundation of being in authority is to be *under* authority.[28] Authority is not based on giving orders; authority is based on obedience. Authority is always given from above, and it is always based on loyalty and obedience to those above you.[29] Giving orders is part of the job, but do not worry; you will learn that soon enough. Everybody can learn to give orders, and in fact, you have already been doing that."

That made me think. "I have never thought about it this way before."

"You have never lived in a kingdom before. This is the way a kingdom functions—well, at least this is the way a kingdom ought to function. In a kingdom, the king must always depend on the obedience and loyalty of his servants. Without that, the kingdom will just become a tyranny. Or, if the king is weak, the kingdom will turn over to anarchy. In the same way, every master in the kingdom also depends on the faithfulness and loyalty of those under his rule, while these rulers themselves exercise their power in obedience and faithfulness to the king. Every ruler who has not learned obedience and loyalty to his king will always rule over his own servants by his pride and for his own interest and pleasure, and thus become a tyrant. On the other hand, however, in the eyes of disobedient and disloyal servants, every ruler will always be a tyrant, even if he is the humblest man on earth and ruling in obedience and faithfulness to his king."[30]

After he allowed me to meditate on his words a few moments, he continued: "So, I am giving you the authority, and I expect you, as a loyal servant, to accept that in obedience. I chose you because of your loyalty—because of your character—not because of your capacity to give orders."

I understood that it was of no use to try further arguments. Then he gave me some more specific instructions, and from that time on, the new order was a fact.

After I went out of his presence, it took me some time of meditating before I could grasp the reality of the new situation. As I reflected on all the implications, I could see now that he had been much more aware of the level of loyalty of his stewards than I had thought. He must indeed have considered that very serious. Just think of what a radical, far-reaching decision it was for him to prefer a young Hebrew slave over older, experienced Egyptian men to become the overseer of such a distinguished place in this country!

The time that followed was not easy. The challenges with the other slaves, their attitudes toward me—it was all just like I had expected. They obeyed me, but the whole situation was constantly stressful to me. In the beginning, the majority of the slaves did not show any loyalty and seemed to enjoy every occasion when I made a mistake or forgot something. I tried to be good to them and to create a pleasant and friendly environment. I understood their hardships very well. I had been in the same situation as them, and just like me, many of them had been sold against their will at some point in their lives. I started to realize that their opposing and challenging attitudes toward me were often just a reflection and the result of their sadness and bitterness. Often, when I saw their faces, I could see the trouble and affliction in their eyes. Sometimes I asked them what was going on. "Nothing," they would usually answer.

However, little by little, I succeeded in winning their confidence—that of a number of them, at least. They started sharing some very sad stories, which gave me the opportunity to comfort them and share a little bit about my own story, how YHWH had helped me overcome the same hardships that they were going through. I did my very best to keep focused on the "marker on the horizon," making use of every opportunity to be a blessing to them. However, to those who rejected me, I was never successful at transmitting my goodwill, and I realized how true the words of my master were when he had said that in the eyes of the disloyal, I would always be a tyrant.

My own loyalty was always first to my master. I felt it was a huge responsibility that he had trusted me with overseeing all he had, and I did not want to make him ashamed for any price. Every time I gave my reports about the slaves, no matter how sorry I sometimes felt, especially for the younger ones, I would never cover up their faults, even though I knew that they could suffer severe consequences. And no matter the fear that I still felt of some of the older slaves, I would never cover up their faults and dishonesty either, even though I knew that they would give me a very hard time during the master's next absence. They would be angry, uncooperative, and disrespectful toward me, and they would do everything they could to make me look bad in the eyes of the master.

One day, one of them said, "Hey, Hebrew, do not make any illusions for yourself! Do not think you will inherit the master's homestead; you will die as poor as you came." It was like déjà vu! Where had I heard that before? *"Hey, dreamer, do not make any illusions for yourself about Father's inheritance. You will surely die in this pit!"*

My brothers always thought that my faithfulness to Father was motivated by my expectation of becoming his heir. Were they right? Was there some truth in that? I remember that I was sometimes not completely sure about that myself.

"Search me, O Elohim, and know my heart," I had prayed. *"Try me, and know my thoughts, and see if there be any wicked way in me."* Was Elohim answering that prayer? Was He trying me, revealing the true motives of my loyalty and faithfulness? Was it for that reason that He had replaced my father with Potiphar? To try me and see if I would be faithful and loyal to a master from whom I could not expect any inheritance or reward? Was it for that reason that I had so many feelings for Potiphar that were similar to those I had had for Father?

Was that the reason I experienced so many attitudes from my fellow slaves that were similar to those I had had from my brothers—their jealousy, their interpretation of why I behaved the way I did, my impotence to do anything good in their eyes? Was everything that had happened to me then really the will and design of Elohim?

"Is that the reason why You have led me all the way through this desert of affliction? To test me, to reveal what is really in my heart? Indeed, O *YHWH*, Your thoughts and Your ways are as high as the heavens, but even so, today You have allowed me to see a glimpse of them!"

In time, I felt that things were improving. As I tried to be righteous, diligent, and faithful toward the master, I felt more and more loved and trusted by him. I could tell that he was satisfied with me—not so much because he would make many affirming comments, but I noticed that he became very...what shall I say? *Unconcerned*. That is the word. He became very unconcerned about everything. He would leave for several days without giving me any instructions, assuming that I knew what to do. Then he would come back after a long trip without asking me how things had been going, assuming that everything was well and that I had it all under control.

Likewise, as I tried to be loving and righteous toward my fellow servants, even though I was demanding and strict, I felt more and more respected by them—even by some of those who had been giving me so much opposition. Many of them almost seemed to forget that I was not Egyptian. Well, I probably also looked, sounded, and acted more and more like an Egyptian, and I do not mean that negatively in any way. However, there always remained a group whose hearts I could never win, and sometimes I worried what kind of trouble that could cause me.

Sometimes I remembered my dreams. I still wondered what they had meant and why Elohim had given them to me, but I did not worry about that. I did not *want* to worry about that. My brothers used to call me a dreamer.[31] I surely did not want to be a dreamer, and I hope that no one will ever think of me as a dreamer. I am sure that you can see now that *YHWH* had taught me it was not His purpose for me to seek the fulfillment of my dreams. His purpose for me was that I would be a blessing to those around me.

As years passed by, I experienced *YHWH* fulfilling that purpose in me. Without sensing any reason for pride but solely for humble gratitude for His grace, I could see that from the day I had become the overseer of my master's house, *YHWH* had blessed his house through me.[32] And by the grace of *YHWH*, I felt true and sincere happiness about that. There were no feelings of "I should be the one receiving the blessing, because it is by my diligence, effort, and faithfulness that things are going so well here"—no feelings of unrighteousness or that I deserved to see my dreams fulfilled.

No. I decided I would not worry about the fulfillment of my own dreams anymore; I would even forget about my dreams.

"You are truly El Shaddai. You are powerful to fulfill the dreams. You do not need my help. I will faithfully work on fulfilling what You want from me, to be a blessing to everyone in every place where you take me. And if I ever worry about the fulfillment of dreams again, let it not be about mine; let it be about the dreams of others."

Chapter 3

The Prison

Imprisoned

The master had left very early that day, and he would be gone for a good number of days. I was doing my routine of attending the usual business in the house when I noticed the master's wife walking toward me. She never traveled with her husband; she was never involved in any of his businesses and responsibilities. In our shepherd culture, the wives were always fully involved in everything their husbands were busy with, and I had always thought of that as normal.

Once, at the beginning of my time at Potiphar's house, I had made a comment about this to some of the other slaves with whom I had become well acquainted.

"Does he never take his wife on his trips?"

"No," they responded, as if this was a very stupid question. "You do not understand. The boss does not have time for that; he is very busy on his trips. He has many difficult and important affairs to take care of."

"Well," I thought, "would that not rather be reason to ask her to join him, to help and support him in all these responsibilities and difficult tasks?" But I did not say anything; I did not want to come across as a wiseacre.

My father, and especially my grandfather, had often explained to me that Elohim Himself had instituted marriage. They taught me that the first and most important purpose for it was that man and wife would work together to serve Him with all their hearts, souls, and strength in whatever they did, in word or in deed.[1] A man would always need the help and support of his wife to do his work, as well as her wisdom and advice to make decisions and fulfill his responsibilities. It surprised me that people of such a high civilization as Egypt seemed to totally lack that understanding, and oftentimes I wondered what the reason for marriage really was for them, apart from having children, of course.

During the times of the master's absence, his wife did not take the responsibility of directing the homestead; that was my job. Every slave, however, including me, respected her and considered that she was entitled to give us commands at her pleasure, and occasionally she would do so. Therefore, this day, when I saw her coming to me, I expected that she wanted to give me some orders. It surprised me that she was alone; her maids were not with her. In addition, she had dressed somewhat provocatively, although I did not pay attention to that at the moment. You would not need to pay much attention, though, to notice that she was a very attractive young woman.

I do not want to get into many details about what happened next; what it comes down to is that she tried to seduce me. She did not see anything wrong with it.

The Prison

She reasoned that her husband would never find out, so what harm could it be to him? I tried to make her understand that I would be betraying the master's trust in me. Above all, I explained, I would be sinning against God, and I would never choose to do anything that would be sorrowful to Him. She could not see it that way, she said, so we stopped arguing, and I left.

However, the following days, she kept insisting. One day, she became so insistent that she pulled me by my coat. I knew that I was in great danger now, and the only thing I could do was leave my coat and run away. She started yelling very loudly, and when some of the slaves came to see what was happening, she showed them my coat.

"Look what that Hebrew did!" she said, as she made up the story that I had been the one wanting to lie with her and that I had fled when she started yelling. Her "proof" was my coat in her hands.

I knew that I was in trouble.

"*That Hebrew,*" she said.

That was music to the ears of those who were still opposed to my stewardship and to whom it was always a thorn in the flesh to be submissive to a Hebrew. They would surely take the fullest advantage of the situation and be very happy to confirm the words of the woman. They would use this affair in their attempts to convince the master that he had been wrong in putting a Hebrew in charge.

On the other hand, I trusted that Elohim, El Shaddai, was on my side. I still believed in hope against hope that He would do something and that with His help, somehow this nightmare would end well for me. It really took only a few days until the master returned, but it seemed like an eternity to me. Even though I was greatly fearful to see his face, I wished he would come home soon so that this time of insecurity about my fate would come to an end.

During those days, I had great difficulty doing my daily work. I could not concentrate on my responsibilities. I could hardly give the orders, and whenever any of the slaves came to me with questions, I just told him to do what he thought was best. I went through a thousand rehearsals of my meeting with the master and prepared myself to explain what had happened. My version of that story would totally contradict what he would hear from his wife and from the other slaves. How would I word it? How could I tell him the truth without offending his own wife, without saying that she was unfaithful, a deceiver…a liar? Oh, my mind was constantly occupied preparing my defense and memorizing the answers to the questions I imagined the master would ask me.

It turned out to be totally useless. The evening the master came home, his wife and the servants wasted neither time nor opportunity to present their story. By the time I was called to see him, his anger was so fierce that I hardly had a chance to speak. It seemed that their testimony, supported by the evidence, was so incriminating that there was no need to hear what I had to say. He shouted at me and expressed his deep disappointment that I had abused his trust in me in such a shameless way. Then he called his officers, who took me away and threw me in prison.

This is how the worst night of my life began. This whole time, the days of waiting for Potiphar to come home, encountering his fierce reaction, me being violently thrown into the prison, feeling my feet being locked in—it all seemed very unreal to me. I could hardly tell if I was dreaming or awake. I had some strange hope that I would suddenly wake up from this terrible dream and get up to continue my job at my master's homestead. As you might suspect, this never happened.

That night, I could not sleep, as the pain of the chains on my feet did not allow me to find a position comfortable enough to rest;[2] I hardly breathed because of the terrible smell of the cold night air. That was when I finally realized, once again: It is real, it is true. I am really here. I am a prisoner in Egypt.

The following days went by slowly. They seemed to last forever; and the nights were even longer. Down there, there was not much difference between day and night anyway; they were almost equally dark. All the time I thought, "How long is this going to be? Is there any hope that these terrible circumstances will end any time soon?" But at the same time, I feared that what would come next could be even more terrible.

One morning, I could hear some officers entering. "Cut him loose," they commanded the chief of the prison. I thought that they were coming for me, but they took one of the other prisoners with them. He never came back. I do not know what happened to him, although I can guess it with nearly complete certainty. After that, many days went by without anything happening at all.

I should tell you that the prison was actually at Potiphar's house.[3] It was built partly under the ground, almost like a pit, and we always called it the dungeon.[4] There were more prisons in Egypt, of course, but this was the one where the most feared suspects were kept, especially those who could be a threat to the king or the nation. "The prisoners of the king," they called them.[5] That was not a title of honor; it just meant that they were potentially the most dangerous to and of concern for the king personally. Keeping these suspects was part of Potiphar's responsibilities, he being the chief of security.

Most prisoners did not stay there very long; they were kept until the day of their judgment, which in most cases came fairly soon. Then they were brought out, either to be executed or to be set free, depending on the verdict. Sometimes it took longer before a case could be solved, and in some rare occasions, even a very long time. This was especially true for cases in which there were no witnesses, the witnesses contradicted each other, or when the witnesses had poor reputations and the king did not trust their testimonies. Those prisoners would stay for an extended period of time, and they usually thought that everybody had forgotten about them.

Even though keeping the prisoners was Potiphar's responsibility, he himself came to the dungeon very rarely—almost never, really. All of us at Potiphar's house were aware of the dungeon, obviously, but most of us never had anything to do with it. He had assigned a chief of prison, which was a respected but undesired position among the slaves. Everybody knew that it was a dark, dirty, smelly place, and nobody envied the task of being in charge of it, having to clean it, and having to hear the prisoners curse constantly.

In the beginning of my imprisonment, I sometimes wondered if Potiphar would be doing anything to investigate my case. Although the apparent proof against me was very strong, there must have been some doubt somewhere in his mind. Otherwise, why would he not yet have executed me? What greater offense can there be to a man than someone trying to take his wife? No man of his rank would allow a slave who had so flagrantly disrespected and so deeply humiliated him to live even one more day! Furthermore, I still believed that, deep in his heart, my master was very sad that he had lost me as his steward.

These thoughts caused a little flame of hope to remain inside me for a long time—hope that one day I would be called out to hear that I had been declared innocent. However, many months went by, and nothing happened. Most likely, Potiphar had never been able to decide what to do with me, and as time went on, his memories of me were buried under the load of his daily responsibilities and troubles. Would everybody just forget about me? Would I remain there the rest of my life, sitting with my feet in these chains?

The Battle

From my first days in prison, I had tried hard to continue in the same spirit that I had learned to operate in during my life as a slave. I meditated on *YHWH*, on how He had showed me the way during my earlier struggles, from the time I came to Egypt. I remembered how He had shown me that He was surely El Shaddai, sovereign over all my circumstances, and that He surely had a purpose for my affliction. I had been able to see this and, to a certain measure, even understand it.

For many days, weeks, and months, I called on, cried out to *YHWH*. And even though I did not hear an answer, I kept alive the hope that something would happen. "I have gone through affliction before," I told myself, "and the same Elohim who led me through valleys of the shadow of death in the past will also help me go through this one."

However, as nothing happened, my pain and the hopelessness of my situation caused in me a slowly increasing frustration, which eventually drove me to desperation. The certainty of His presence that did not depend on feelings...the security that He was always with me despite the fact I did not see or feel any evidence—it had all been so real to me. But now it started to dissipate.

"Why do You not answer? Where are You? My Elohim, why have You forsaken me?"

Then there were times when I thought that He was answering, especially when I recalled the many stories of my father's and grandfather's hardships or the memories of the times of my own trials and when He had delivered me. During those moments, these stories and memories helped me and caused me to feel that my faith and trust in Him were being restored.

But then again, doubts and darkness would come over me and increase until they overwhelmed me as a great wave, overwriting my thoughts of hope with arguments of unbelief. They "showed" me that I was just trying to console myself—that I was just making up the thoughts and feelings that Elohim was answering, trying to produce my own peace. They told me that it was just my imagination—that it was not real.

"What is the foundation for your belief?" they challenged me. "What evidence and proof are there that *YHWH* is real? The stories of your fathers? That is no proof at all! They just made up their stories to console themselves the same way you do. The blessings they received from Elohim? So what? The Egyptians receive just as many blessings as the Hebrews. Your uncle Esau is just as blessed as your father, and your great-uncle Ishmael is just as blessed as your grandfather. Chosen by Elohim? Every nation believes it is the beloved of its god."

I hated these arguments, but I could not stop them. They had so much evidence, while I had no substance to contradict them. I felt no ground beneath my feet at all anymore—no foundation to stand on. Where was this going? I felt myself falling in a pit without bottom. I kept falling and falling, deeper and deeper, and my thoughts were becoming even darker than this prison.

What about Potiphar? I had felt such a strong conviction that *YHWH* had appointed me to be a blessing to him. I had learned to love him, to be loyal and faithful to him. Although he was the cause that I could not return to my father, I had never held that against him; I had always thought of him as a righteous person. But look how he treated me! How could he have done this to me?

I started hating him and talking to him in my imagination.

"Righteous? You are the most selfish person I have ever known. You only think of yourself! Your next meal is the only thing you care about![6] How much have I suffered for you, given up for you? How often have I stood up in favor of you before your own servants, defending your honor and reputation without you even knowing it? I have served you and honored you as a king, even though I knew that I would never get anything in return. I knew that I would die as poor as I came, but that never kept me from seeking the best for you. I always rejoiced in seeing your fields producing in abundance and your horses shining as mirrors. It made me feel happy to hear people commending you for the beautiful condition of your homestead, even if nobody ever gave me any credit for it. I was satisfied and happy with just being able to be a blessing to you. I do not expect you to give me thanks, but why did you have to return me evil and insult for blessing?"

What about the Egyptians? I had desired to be a blessing to them as well. I had believed that El Shaddai had sovereignly brought me here to bless them, to console those who were suffering. How many times had I lent a listening ear to them? How many times had I looked at their faces—noticed the sadness in their eyes—and shown interest and care, even if they were hardly willing to share their burdens with me? How many times had I heard stories that they had never before told anyone? Had I not always been there for them? And what had I expected in return? Nothing.

"I just desired to be a blessing to you. I believed that *YHWH* was also your God—that He also loved you, even if you did not know Him or love Him, even if you were not His chosen. I believed that I was chosen to make Him known to you so that you also might know Him—*YHWH* your Creator, the true God of the heavens. And what did you do to me? You are liars, deceivers, hypocrites; you have opened your wicked and deceitful mouths against me and spoken against me with a lying tongue.[7] You are not trustworthy; you reward me evil for good and hatred for love. You are all criminals; you should all be in this dungeon. You do not deserve the mercy of *YHWH*. I wish He would bring a famine so bad that you and your entire land would perish! That is what you deserve! You think of yourselves as the top of the world, and you do not know that you are the very vilest and lowest."

And what about Elohim? I feared to allow my mind to birth any disrespectful thought, but I was not sure what to believe about Him anymore.

"I know that You exist, that You are out there somewhere. But I have immense trouble calling You 'the One who lives and sees me.' Maybe You see me, maybe you hear me, but what difference does it make if You do not do anything anyway? Must the thought that you watch and see me console me? Does that not hurt me even more? Would it not be better to believe that You have forgotten about me, or that You have fallen asleep, or do not even exist, than to believe that You are watching me and letting me down intentionally? What is the purpose of treating me like this? Why do You choose me if You do not have any purpose for my life anyway? Why do You give me dreams and promises if none of that is ever really going to happen to me? Why do You give me understanding of Your truth if nothing is ever going to happen *according* to Your truth? Why do You teach me Your ways if You never guide me according to Your ways? Why do You lead me, but I never end up where You promise to take me?"

Although deep in my heart I did not want to think these thoughts, I could no longer fight against them. I was exhausted. They were so strong; they had so much proof, so much evidence, and such undeniable arguments. Would there ever stand up a deliverer with the power to defeat them?

The Victory

One morning, as I tried to change my position, I was confronted again with the reality that I could hardly move with those chains on my feet, and despair got me in its grip again. As always, my thoughts wanted to take this opportunity and started boasting again. This time, however, they were immediately silenced.

"Who is this who darkens counsel by words without knowledge?[8] Is it right for you to be angry?"[9]

The rebuke shook me up. It was a voice in my mind that sounded firm and convicting, but patient and loving at the same time.

"What about Potiphar?" the voice continued. "Yes, you learned to love him, and you were loyal to him despite not expecting any reward or heritage. But was that not under condition of him being righteous? What if he made a mistake? What if he preferred another over you? What if he believed another instead of you? What if he offended you? Or what if he were not as righteous as you thought? Does that give you the right to withdraw your loyalty? Is he not your master even when he is wrong?"

I knew that *YHWH* was answering me, but this was not the kind of answer that I desired. I had hoped for a more compassionate answer, one that would agree with my hurt feelings—one with the same compassion I felt for myself. I wanted an answer that would confirm that I was right while others were wrong and evil, an answer that would sweeten the bitterness in my heart.

"Do You mean that my attitude toward Potiphar, my attitude of humility and respect...do You mean that *that* attitude was still full of pride? Do You mean that my loyalty and faithfulness were still largely motivated by my selfishness and self-righteousness? I know that I prayed *'Search me, O Elohim, and know my heart; try me, and know my thoughts.'*[10] But I thought You had done that already; I thought You were through. I thought that You had reached in and revealed the secrets of my heart and that You had found me perfect—a faithful servant, a loyal slave. But now I see that You are opening a whole new pit beneath that, uncovering a whole new layer in my heart, a reality that I had never seen and that You had not shown me yet."

I started to understand that *YHWH* expected more from me. Yes, I had been faithful to my master, but now He was showing me that I had set limits and conditions. "How far do You expect me to go? How many times do You expect me to forgive? How deeply do You expect me to humble myself? How far must I go in denying myself?" As I reflected on my attitudes, I realized that I had not been as humble and loving as I thought I had. The more I meditated and the more I sensed the rebuke from Elohim, the more I could see my own selfishness. I knew that *YHWH* was not punishing me for anything that I had done wrong. Actually, I had never felt that—not even when I was sold and taken to Egypt. But I started to understand that there were still many areas in my heart where He wanted to change me, areas that I had never been aware of.

So, yes, what about Potiphar? "Potiphar, my master, maybe you did the right thing. What would I have done if I were in your shoes? What could you have done? You could not possibly have chosen to trust me more than you trust your own wife. And even if what you did was not the right thing...even if you did wrong...even if you were unrighteous to me, I am not your judge. I forgive you. I will remain loyal and faithful to you as long as I am your slave. You can trust me. I will honor you and serve you in whatever you ask of me. Well, at this point, I have no choice; I cannot choose whether to remain with my feet in these chains or not. But this will be the attitude of my heart. Or, I should say, I will keep working on it to *make* this the attitude of my heart. If you ever give me a task again, I promise that this will be the attitude with which I will serve you. I will be your loyal slave and faithful servant, no matter what, without any conditions. You can count on me. Today I return to you, my master, and submit myself under your hand."[11]

What about the Egyptians? "Is it right for you to be so angry at the Egyptians? If they are all liars, deceivers, and criminals, is that then not the very reason why they need Me? Would you only be willing to love and bless them if they were good people, at least not any worse than you? Anyone would be able to love them if they were all good people. If you love only those who treat you well, does not anyone in Egypt do the same?[12] Were you not chosen to be different? Were you not chosen to make Me known among them? So, what do you teach them about Me? Do you really know Me? What do you think of Me? How am I? Am I like you? Do I think the way you think? Are My thoughts not higher than yours?[13] Is it not time, then, for you to forsake your own thoughts and to learn to think My thoughts?"

I knew very well that my arguments had told me a lot of nonsense, even lies, but in my frustration and bitterness, I had let them dwell in my mind and even allowed them to direct and control my thoughts. I knew very well that not all Egyptians were criminals—actually, very few were. But even if they were, what difference did it make?

"I will forgive them; I am not their judge," I decided. "I was brought here to be a blessing to them, to serve them, even to love them and help in their needs and trouble, unconditionally."

That morning, I made a promise. "If I ever have the opportunity again to serve even one of you Egyptians, I will do so with all my heart. Even if you are a criminal, I will treat you and honor you and serve you as a king. I will do all that is in me to understand your needs. I will rejoice in your prosperity even if I suffer adversity, and I will rejoice in your deliverance even if I remain in bonds."

And what about Elohim?

Even though I had said that I would forget about my dreams, I saw now that they still bothered me. It was not so much the fact that the wonderful things I had hoped for and believed in based on the dreams had not come true; I had learned to accept that. What bothered me deep inside was what I would think of Elohim if it seemed to me that He did not fulfill what He had said and promised. Could I still believe that He was faithful and true? How could I recover my trust in Him? What would my response be the next time He said or promised something? Would I have faith in Him and in His words? What would that faith be based on?

Then I asked myself, "Can there be darkness in Him? Is it right for me to judge the eternal One according to *my* wisdom and righteousness?"

Acknowledging my error, I cried out to Elohim. "O *YHWH*, I know that I have made a fool of myself. I have allowed myself to think bitter thoughts about You. But deep in my heart, I know that You are true; there cannot be lies in You. Your thoughts are higher than my thoughts. Therefore, teach me to think your thoughts; help me to understand Your ways."

Had I thought my own thoughts about His dreams? Could that have caused my confusion? Had I dreamed His dreams but consulted my own thoughts concerning their meaning and fulfillment?

"Have I been judging You and putting expectations on You based on my own thoughts and understanding?" That morning, I bowed my head and asked for *YHWH*'s forgiveness. I knew that I had been a fool. I abhorred myself and repented in dust and ashes. "I know that it is *me* who darkens counsel by words without knowledge. I have thought and spoken things that I did not understand, things too wonderful for me, which I did not know. I need You to teach me, to instruct me. I will ask; I need You to answer me.[14] From now on, I will accept that not only are my dreams Yours, but also the meanings, the interpretations, and the answers are Yours. I know and recognize that You are faithful and true. I will not remind You of what You promised me according to my own understanding. Rather, I will always trust and believe that You are faithful and true to fulfill Your plans and promises.

"This morning, I do not come before You to remind You of the dreams and promises You have given me, or to tell You what I expect and wish from You. Instead, I come before You to ask what You expect from me. I promise You that from now on, I will always stand before You as a humble learner with the desire to understand Your thoughts, and as a loyal servant with the desire to obey Your commands."

Walking in Freedom

That morning, the world changed. I experienced the presence of *YHWH* restored to me. I knew that He was with me. The roles were reversed. It was no longer me expecting *YHWH* to fulfill His promises. Now it was *YHWH* expecting *me* to fulfill the promise that *I* had made. From that day on, I stood before Him every morning and asked Him to help me to fulfill and live out that promise.

As I told Him that I wanted to serve Him and asked Him to guide me, more opportunities presented themselves than I could ever have imagined. All this time, I had kept the perspective that I could not do anything; I was bound in chains. I could not move or go anywhere. But now, as I stopped thinking about my own misery, my whole outlook started to change.

Suddenly, I realized that I was not the only one who was suffering. I started seeing the needs of those around me. In the midst of the darkness, I rediscovered the bright light of understanding as I realized that El Shaddai had never changed, nor had He changed His mind. I was still chosen by Him, chosen to be a blessing. Now I realized that He had never deprived me of opportunities to reach that purpose and destiny! I could see now how many needs there were around me, many ways in which I could be a blessing. In fact, probably never before had I been in circumstances where I had so many opportunities to help, support, and comfort! I saw that the enslavement to my own dreams and desires had been the only impediment to my serving *YHWH* and walking according to His calling. The only prison that had deprived me of the freedom that I needed to reach His purpose and destiny for my life had been the bonds of my selfishness!

From that day on, I was able to walk free again. The feet of my body were still locked in chains, but the feet of my soul had never been as free before. As I walked in this newness of mind, my outward attitude changed accordingly. I tried to do everything I could to create a friendly, more pleasant environment. Well, I admit that anyone, including myself, would consider it ridiculous to think that place could be friendly and pleasant. So, to be realistic, you must interpret these terms in a relative sense. But I just decided to believe Elohim that with His help, I could be a blessing and make a difference there in a similar way that, by His grace, the environment at Potiphar's homestead had changed when I had taken this same attitude.

With this new attitude, I started talking with the other prisoners. At first, they just rejected any manifestation of kindness. But little by little, they started responding. I understood their hardships very well. I was in the same situation as they were, and just like me, some could have been innocent and had no way of proving it. Some of them shared some very hard stories about unrighteousness committed against them. This gave me the opportunity to comfort them and share a little bit of my own story—especially how *YHWH* had helped me overcome the same hardships they were going through. I did my very best to keep focused on the "marker on the horizon" and to make use of every opportunity to be a blessing to them.

I know that the chief of the prison also noticed the change in my attitude—mainly because I became much friendlier toward him, but also because he overheard the conversations that I had with the other prisoners.

One day, he said, "You should help me run this place."

A bit surprised, I responded, "I would be glad to do so, but it is a little hard with these chains."

"You know what? I will loosen your chains so that you can help me to clean this place out."

"Do you think that Potiphar will approve of that?"

"Why not, as long as you do not try to escape? You know what will happen to me if a prisoner under my care escapes, right?" he asked.

"I will be as faithful to you as I was—as I *am*—to the master."

He did not answer, and I wondered what he thought. That would depend on whether he believed me to be guilty or not. I had already decided not to talk about that anymore—not with him or the other prisoners either. I understood that it was wrong to do that, because it always provoked a wave of insults against Potiphar and everyone else who represented the king. Insulting the king was their favorite topic all the time anyway, and I was determined to be very careful not to give more food for these conversations. It would not make any difference anyway what the prison keeper thought. He was not my judge; he was just another slave.

It felt very different to be able to walk freely inside the prison. It took some time for my feet and the rest of my body to respond, but after that, I was soon doing basically all the work there—bringing food to each prisoner and cleaning the place where they were sitting. That was not a desirable or honorable job for any slave, but for me, it was surely a big promotion from where I had been since I had been taken in there.

Whatever the prison keeper thought of my being guilty or not, I could tell that he trusted me. He did not say so, but I could see that he became very unconcerned about everything. He hardly gave me any instructions; he just trusted that I knew what to do and that I would do it. Sometimes I would not see him for days. Some of the new prisoners who had arrived after I was freed from my chains even seemed to think that this was my job as a slave; they hardly realized that I was also a prisoner. The only way they could tell the difference was that I did not have my hair and beard shaved off.

Do not misunderstand me—I never grew to like it there. Far from it! The desire of my heart to be released from this pit never faded, and even though the odds seemed very unfavorable, I always kept this little flame of hope burning inside me that someday the gate would swing open and my name would be called.

The Officers

"Hurry up! Potiphar is at the gate waiting for you!" the prison keeper shouted as he came running down to me. "The master is here; he wants to talk with you!"

The master was here! Not an officer or a steward, but the master himself! And he wanted to talk with me! That was good news! It felt as if a can of oil was poured on that little flame of hope. This must be the day!

"What does he want to tell me?"

Thousands of thoughts flashed through my mind during the few moments that it took me to walk up to the gate. Would he tell me that he had found me innocent? Would he have evidence that his wife was not faithful to him? Would she have confessed the truth, or at least spoken in favor of me, no longer being able to carry the burden of guilt over me being an innocent prisoner? And what would he do with me? Would he restore me to my old position? Or send me home to Canaan? Had it been enough now in the eyes of *YHWH*? Would today be as the day when Elohim had spoken to my great-grandfather, when He had said, *"Enough, for now I know that you fear Me"*?[15]

"Have You tried my faithfulness, and has it been enough? O my Elohim, I know that Your mercies endure forever!"

When I came to the gate, I saw my master standing, waiting for me. I did not look at his face; I could only see his silhouette anyway because of the bright daylight behind him. He called me by my name, and then he said, "I need your service."

The Prison

"Yes, Master?"

"We have two new prisoners. They are very important men, high officers of the king. We do not know if they are guilty; they may very well be innocent. But while we are investigating, they must remain in prison. Until we know for sure, I want them to be treated well, with due respect. I am very concerned about the thought that we could be treating innocent high officers as if they were criminals, so I want you to take care of them.[16] I want you to give them the best possible care and environment, as far as the circumstances allow. I trust that I can count on you."

"Yes, Master, of course, you can count on me."

"Well, then, they will be here shortly." Then he turned around and left.

I also turned and went back to my duties, but I could not attend to the other prisoners the way they had gotten used to. I did not talk; my mind was so busy processing the confusion. The burning fire of hope had lasted only a short while, but it had been so intense that it could not be simply quenched in an instant. It had left a huge heap of ashes, a very deep and painful wound.

"Of course, Master, I know that you are very concerned about the thought that you could be treating innocent people as if they were criminals. That must be the reason why you treat me the way you do, right?" That whole day, I walked around carrying on internal conversations, talking to myself, to *YHWH*, and to the master. I only vaguely remember helping the prison keeper put the two new prisoners in their chains and noticing that these high officers looked very humiliated. As for the rest, the memories of everything that happened that day are covered up by my own thoughts and feelings.

What came next was another one of those long, sleepless nights—another battle: arguments about the master's unrighteousness and hypocrisy, about Egyptian criminals, and about why El Shaddai had given me a flame of hope—another dream of sorts—and then stamped it out again. This time, however, my war against my own thoughts and arguments took a very different course from those in the past. I fought back. I responded firmly and bravely, "No! I will not follow you. I will not submit to you; you will not take me back into your prison. I have another Master, He has set me free and only Him I will serve. I will be faithful and loyal to Him. I will take every one of you into captivity in obedience to Him."[17]

Once again, I cried out to YHWH for help, and He responded. With His help, I responded in my mind to the master. I remembered the night when I had committed myself to him, when I had said, *"Potiphar, my master...I forgive you. I will remain loyal and faithful to you as long as I am your slave. You can trust me. I will honor you and serve you in whatever you ask of me...If you ever give me a task again, I promise that this will be the attitude with which I will serve you. I will be your loyal slave and faithful servant."*

"Yes, Master. You can count on me," I repeated, but this time with all my heart. I committed to dedicating myself to the fullest to carry out the task he had given me. I would serve these men whom he had put under

The Prison

my care to the best of my abilities and honor them as kings.[18]

I also remembered the night I had committed myself to the people of Egypt. "*If I ever have the opportunity again to serve even one of you Egyptians, I will do so with all my heart. Even if you are a criminal, I will treat you and honor you and serve you as a king. I will do all that is in me to understand your needs. I will rejoice in your prosperity even if I suffer adversity, and I will rejoice in your deliverance even if I remain in bonds.*"

Then, by the grace of Elohim, I responded in my mind to these two officers. "Maybe you both are criminals; I do not know. But I am not your judge; I am your servant, brought to you to be a blessing. You can count on me."

And with the help of *YHWH*, I responded to Him. "Was it really You who gave me this short dream of being released from this pit this morning? Or was it me again? Honestly, I recognize that, once again, it was my own interpretation. Help me to learn from You. The interpretations are Yours. Teach me not to darken the counsel by words without knowledge. Teach me to ask and to wait for You to answer." Then I fell asleep.

Even though the morning came very soon, I felt rested to begin the day. The following days, I returned to my routine of taking care of my people. I gave extra attention to the two officers—not because I wanted to be partial, but because that had been my master's order. I found out that they were the chief cupbearer and the chief baker of Pharaoh. These were considered very high positions; they were men of confidence, very close to the king. I wondered what they were suspected of. Had they tried to poison the food or the wine? I never asked; it was none of my business. I could tell that they felt very embarrassed to be under these circumstances and among people of such a different class. They were silent, and when they talked at all, it was usually just in low voices between the two of them. They did not curse and complain loudly as most others did. They were very well-educated people, totally out of place in this prison.

One morning, I came to them to serve them as usual. When I looked at them and I saw their faces, despite the darkness of the dungeon, I immediately noticed something different.

"Are you well?" I asked.

"Yes, we are well—or as well as one can be under these circumstances," the cupbearer answered. "Thank you for asking."

"So why then do your faces look so sad?"

"Well, what do you expect?" he replied. "How many happy faces do you see here?"

"Sir, I do not want to insist, but with all due respect, I want you to know that I see your faces every day, of both of you. And I see that you are different today than yesterday and all the days before since you have been here. I believe that something happened or that something different is going on with both of you."[19]

I could see that they were surprised. At the king's court, they were well trained not to allow their countenances to show their feelings, and they almost seemed to consider it a humiliation that I had discovered them.

"Well, then, you are right. Something did happen last night. We both had dreams, and here, there is no interpreter."

A dream! My heart called out to *YHWH*, "O my Elohim! What am I supposed to say? 'A dream? Do not pay attention to dreams. I also had a dream, and look where I am! Dreams do not mean anything; they bring only false hopes!'" This is *not* what I said, but I have no doubt that this would have been my response if I had retained bitterness in my heart about my unfulfilled dreams and desires—if *YHWH* had not healed me and helped me to overcome those selfish attitudes. Now, so many years later, as I look back and remember that day, I understand that my true attitude toward Him, the Giver of the dreams, was being tried and revealed.

So what *did* I say? At first, I really did not know how to respond. How could I honestly take their dreams seriously when I did not even understand what to think of my own dreams? How could I say that their dreams meant anything if sometimes I was not even sure anymore whether my own dreams had any meaning at all? Would that not be hypocrisy? Oh, why a dream? Had they said anything else, I would have been able to respond. Had they told me that their feet were hurting, I could have talked with the chief of the prison about some kind of temporary relief. Had they been worried about their families, I could have helped them by finding someone to send a message to them. Why a dream?

When my spirit calmed down, I remembered what *YHWH* had been teaching me about dreams and how I had been responding and committing myself. What had I said? *"If I ever worry about the fulfillment of dreams again, let it not be about mine; let it be about the dreams of others."* And what had He taught me about what was not being fulfilled? Were they my dreams, or my own *interpretations* of the dreams? Had that not been my problem? Had I not been putting expectations on Elohim according to my own selfish and self-centered interpretations of the dreams?

"O Elohim, do not let me obscure the counsel with words without knowledge and declare things that are too wonderful to me, that I do not understand. I will ask, and You will answer me. Only You—*only You*—know the meaning of the dreams."

Then, without showing any evidence of the battle and confusion that was going on in my mind, I responded:

"An interpreter? I do not think that they exist."

"Well, at the court, we have interpreters of dreams."

Without arguing, calmly, but with total conviction, I responded, "The interpretations belong to God; only God can give the answers." Then, in the hope that *YHWH* would reveal to me His interpretations if they were willing to share their dreams, I continued, "Tell me your dreams."

They looked at each other, and then they said, "All right, then."

The Prison

The cupbearer told his dream first. He had dreamed that he was back in office. He saw himself picking grapes, pressing them into a cup, and serving the cup to the king. Even before he had finished his story, Elohim had already revealed to me what the meaning of the dream was. I knew with certainty that it meant that the cupbearer was going to be declared innocent and that he would return to his office. When I gave him the interpretation from Elohim, I could see the joy in both men's eyes, and I truly rejoiced with them.

Next, the baker told his dream. He was confident that he would get a favorable interpretation as well, because he had also seen himself back in office. "Three white baskets were on my head," he said, "and in the uppermost basket were all kinds of baked goods for the king, and the birds ate them out of the basket on my head." The moment he mentioned the birds, Elohim revealed to me a completely different outcome. It was very hard for me to give him the answer. It truly hurt me to have to tell him that he was going to be executed.

Was he really guilty? I never found out. I never found out if the cupbearer was truly innocent either. I just left that in the hands of El Shaddai. I still had three days to talk with them and take care of them. Was there any hope for the baker? Not in this world, but I knew that one day he would meet another Judge who would make no mistakes nor commit unrighteousness. I counseled the baker to put his trust in Him, to repent of any evil, and to ask forgiveness. I taught him to pray: "Create in me a clean heart, O God, and renew a right spirit within me. Deliver me from the guilt, O God of my salvation."[20]

I asked the cupbearer to speak to the king on my behalf. Was I right to do that? Maybe not. At the time, I thought that maybe Elohim had sent him to prison for a special reason, as an angel for me. What else could the purpose of my encounter with this man have been?

So, after the officers left, every day I again had that little flame of hope that maybe someone would come for me, sent by the king, at least to hear my case. As time passed by and nothing like that ever happened, I started to accept my mission—not by way of resignation, but with joy that surpasses all understanding. Every day, I thanked *YHWH* with all my heart for the privilege of serving Him according to His plan and design.

"If this is Your will for me, if this is the place where You want me, if this is the place where people need me, I will serve You here for the rest of my life," I prayed. "It is well with me. Not my will, but Yours be done. I will be loyal to You, my Master, and therefore, I will remain loyal to Potiphar, my master. I will love the Egyptians and be a blessing to them, even if they are criminals."

Many months passed. Prisoners came and left. When they were taken out, I almost never knew for sure what would happen to them, but I usually had a strong sense of what the verdict was. Those who were guilty often showed a very rebellious attitude, but when they were taken out, when I saw their faces, I could see the despair in their eyes. "Let my advice be acceptable to you," I would counsel them. "Renounce your sins and wickedness.[21] Prepare your heart to meet *YHWH*, your God and Creator, your righteous Judge. Ask Him for forgiveness. Humble yourself before Him. His mercies endure forever." On the few occasions when I knew that a prisoner was declared innocent, I truly rejoiced with him in his deliverance, even though I remained in bonds. This is what I had promised *YHWH*, and He was always faithful to give me the grace to fulfill this promise.

Every morning, I asked *YHWH* to help me be a blessing there. That was the purpose for which *YHWH* had chosen me, and it was for that purpose that He had placed me there. I knew that I was truly fulfilling His calling.

Sometimes I thought about Father. Would he still be alive? Would he still be mourning for me? "Do not cry for me, *Abi*," I imagined myself saying to him.[22] "All is well with me. I am living the promise. *YHWH* is fulfilling the Blessing of Abraham in me and through me. He has blessed me by allowing me to be a blessing to those who need Him the most and who have the least opportunity to hear about Him."

When I Saw Their Faces

Chapter 4

The King's Court

The King's Dream

I was doing my job as usual when I heard the chief of the prison talking with some men at the gate, and I wondered which prisoner would be taken out today. Then I clearly heard one of them mention "Hebrew slave."

"Yes, he is here," the prison keeper answered, "I will bring him out." I heard his footsteps quickly coming down to where I was attending the other prisoners. His voice sounded excited when he said, "Hurry up! You are going to be taken to the king!"

"The king?"

"Do not ask; hurry up! I will finish the work here."

Before I even had a chance to think about what could be going on, I was already outside where two officers were waiting for me. It was evident that they were in great haste to take me to wherever it was we were going. They did not use the same rudeness that I had often seen the prisoners being treated with, nor had they put chains on my hands. Therefore, I did not fear that I was going to be executed. I could not understand why they would take me to the king, though. Was he going to hear me? No, my case could surely not be important enough to be treated by the king personally.

Everything was going much too fast for me to understand what was happening. By the time I got used to the daylight, we had arrived at the king's court. I had never been there before, but I just knew that this had to be the king's court. Then one of the officers told me that the king wanted to talk with me, but first, I was going to be taken to a bathroom to get ready to enter into the king's presence, he explained.

They shaved my head and my beard and gave me clean clothes, and then they took me to the king. I was very nervous and still had no idea what to expect.

The king was sitting on a throne and was surrounded by important-looking people. I understood that they were his most important servants—his trusted men who were closest to him, his counselors and high officers. I recognized the cupbearer who had been with me in prison about two years before. He was standing next to the king, and as soon as he saw me, he whispered something in the king's ear. When I saw the king's face, immediately all my fear was gone. Even though his countenance was serene, I discerned that the intention of this man was not to condemn me.

I must say that the environment in the presence of the king was very different from anything I would have imagined, if I ever had. I was very surprised at the first feeling that came over me as I watched the king's face. If I had expected anything, it would have been a sense of fear. But it was not fear that I felt; rather, it was compassion. I discerned that there was something happening here and that the king was not capable of controlling the situation or solving the problem—or at least that he felt that way.

What also surprised me was that, even though it was very hard to guess his age, it was obvious that he was much younger than one would expect a king to be, and that was without any doubt part of the reason why I felt this compassion. I was led closer to the throne, and when I stood before the king, everyone around him became silent.

Then the king started speaking. "Are you the Hebrew man, slave of my chief of security?"

"Yes, my king, I am." I stood there expectantly as he appeared to consider his words. Then he spoke.

"I dreamed a dream, and none of my counselors have been able to interpret it." He paused, looking at my face as if he was trying to discern my thoughts. Then he continued, "I have heard it said of you that you understand dreams and interpret them."

It took me a moment to realize what was happening. Had they brought me out of the prison and into the presence of the king for this reason—because he had had a dream that he did not understand? This could not be true. I must be the one who was dreaming! Then I noticed the look on the cupbearer's face, and I understood what must have occurred. Surely, the king had told his dream to his counselors and high officers, and the cupbearer must have remembered me from the day Elohim had given me the interpretation of his dream. He must have told the king about me. Therefore, now they had brought me here in the hopes that I could explain the king's dream as well and give him the answers he needed.

Everyone in the court looked at me, waiting to hear what I would say. I began to feel intimidated by the silence and by all the eyes that were watching me. A wave of uncertainty came over me. Would my Elohim really want to reveal His answers for the king to me? I knew He could. Had He not also given me the answers for his officers? On the other hand, had He not also taught me how delicate it is to have my own thoughts about the meaning of dreams—to interpret dreams according to my own understanding? Had He not given me fear to darken counsel by words without knowledge? In the midst of these doubts, I humbly responded, "Understanding dreams is not in me, O King. Not even the wise men, the counselors, and the interpreters can declare the secret that the king demands. But there is a God in heaven who reveals secrets. He will give the answer for the well-being of the king. He is the only One who can."[1]

I knew that my answer could be very disappointing to him, and that made me sad, although not so much for myself. I surely do not want to try to make you believe that I had reached such perfection as to be free from all selfishness, but I honestly felt sad for him, not for myself. I could see in his face that he was very concerned about what he had seen in his dream, and I really wished I could help him and be a blessing to him. What would his reaction be?

"Well, then," I expected to hear him say, "if he cannot understand and interpret the dream, then you may take him back now." I would go back to prison and continue my life, but with another burden—the burden of having stamped out a flame of hope instead of being a blessing. That made me feel sad.

But that was not what he said. Instead, without further comments or questions, he started sharing the dream! It was like he completely ignored what I had said when I told him it was not in me to understand dreams, that only Elohim could reveal these secrets. Or could it be that he believed—or at least hoped—that Elohim would answer him *through me*? If so, then he was right! As soon as he started telling the dream, I knew that *YHWH* was going to reveal its meaning to me.

Without showing it, I rejoiced in my spirit. "O my Elohim, blessed be Your name forever and ever, for wisdom and might are Yours, and You are the One who gives wisdom to the wise and knowledge to those who have understanding.[2] You are surely faithful in giving me the opportunities to fulfill my promise and to serve according to Your purpose! Indeed, nothing is impossible with You. One moment You allow me to be a blessing to a prisoner, and the next moment You allow me to be a blessing to a king."

I listened very carefully to each word of the story. It turned out that the king had had two dreams. "In my dream, I was standing by the Great River," he said. "Suddenly, I saw seven fine-looking fat cows coming out of the water. After them, also seven poor, ugly, and thin cows climbed out of the river. Nowhere in Egypt have I ever seen such ugly cows. As I continued watching, the ugly cows approached the fine cows and devoured each one of them. However, after they had eaten them, they were still as thin as they were before. Then I woke up." All the servants remained completely silent while looking at the king. They were all waiting for him to continue and to share his second dream. "In my second dream, I saw a reed coming up, and seven ears full of grain sprouted from that reed. Then, also seven thin ears came up. They were dry and ugly, as burned by the wind, and these thin ears bent over toward the good ears and devoured them."

While I was listening to the words of the king, I was filled with the understanding that the two dreams were in fact one and the same story, told in two different ways. And by the time he finished speaking, I knew exactly what that story was. Elohim was showing the king what He was going to do very soon in Egypt and in the surrounding nations!

However, the fact that *YHWH* had given me the understanding of the meaning of the dreams produced in me an even greater sadness than the one I had felt before. But this time, the interpretation itself was the cause of my sadness. Elohim had showed me that, after a period of great wealth and prosperity, there was going to come an unprecedented famine so severe that it would totally ravage and consume the land. As I was deeply troubled and feeling profound pain for the king and his people, I realized how much I had learned to love this nation. I remembered that there was a time when I had wished that Elohim would cause the whole of Egypt to perish through a famine, and now that He showed me that He was actually going to do so, it broke my heart.

"O *YHWH*, You know how much I desire to be a blessing to this king and to this nation. It is for that purpose that You have chosen me and prepared me, and it is for that reason that You have brought me here. And now, You are sending me to deliver this message of a curse." There was no way out; I had to tell them.

The eyes of the king and all officers were fixed on me, and everyone was expecting the answer for the well-being of the king. "The dreams of the king mean one and the same thing," I said, starting with some hesitation. "God has shown the king what He is going to do in Egypt. The seven good cows that you saw in your first dream and the seven good ears of grain in your second dream mean the same thing: they represent seven years of great plenty and abundance." I sighed deeply and then continued, "However, the seven lean, ugly cows and the seven empty ears of grain scorched by the wind that came up afterward—they are seven years of famine. That famine will be very grievous. Nothing of the abundance of the first seven years will remain, and the great prosperity will be totally forgotten. The famine will be so severe that it will ravage and consume the entire land of Egypt."

I could see the face of the king and the faces of his servants turn pale out of despair. None of them mistrusted the interpretation; they all had the conviction that this was the true meaning. And then, I had to say one more thing. As the deathblow, I had to add, "And this is going to happen very soon."

As I looked at the king's face, I was deeply moved, filled with compassion. He was so young. It was so obvious to me that he could not possibly have the preparation and experience that he would need to solve the problems that he was going to face. Seven years of famine! "O *YHWH*, my Elohim, what else can I say? What can I do? You have raised this man up as the king of this great nation. I can see that he is greatly overwhelmed by this impossible task of saving his people from such a disaster. Is there anything else I can say or do before they take me back to prison?"

Instantly, a bright thought rose up in my mind. "Now, my king, do not lose hope," I continued, trying to give a hopeful sound to my voice. "Let my king choose a discerning and wise man and set him over the land of Egypt. Then, let this man commission officers in every city and province. These officers will collect the excess of the food production during the seven plentiful years and store up the grain in storehouses. Then that food will be a reserve for the land in the seven years of famine that will come, so that the land of Egypt may not perish."

I knew that I had been very daring in taking the position of the king's counselor. Who, without being asked to do so, would be entitled to lecture the king of Egypt and all his servants and to advise them on what decisions to make? Certainly not a Hebrew prisoner! Moreover, I hoped that the king would take no offense at my counsel—that he would not sense that I underestimated his capacity to care for his country when I advised him to find someone else, a "discerning and wise man," to carry out this responsibility.

I felt greatly relieved when I saw the faces of the king and his servants lighting up. They started talking to one another, and even though I could not discern much of what each person was saying, I saw that all of them were in favor of my proposal. Nobody paid any attention to me anymore, and I took advantage of that to observe their reaction unnoticed.

I was not sure if it was my imagination or my discernment that gave me the impression that several of them considered themselves fairly discerning and wise men and therefore good candidates for this new office. I could not help suspecting that there was potentially some competition and jealousy among them. I had no doubt that they were all very brilliant and wise men; there must have been good reasons for each of them to have become part of this elite group of personal counselors and high officers of the king. They were certainly all educated in the best schools of Egypt, which were probably the best schools in the world.

"Some of them must be great agricultural experts," I thought. "They will be able to make sure that full advantage will be taken from the years of bounty. Others may be architects or construction experts, very well prepared for the job of designing and overseeing the building of large storehouses. Others may have experience in conservation of grain or in organizing and administrating large projects."

It struck me that the king himself did not speak with any of them, nor did anyone talk to him. He just sat there meditating on the situation. I imagined that many names of possible candidates were going through his mind and that he was thinking about which procedure to follow to come to the election of the indicated man.

Then suddenly, he stood up. Everyone was immediately silent and looked at him. "Can we find another man like this man, a man in whom is the Spirit of God?" Next, before anyone even had a chance to respond, he turned to me and said, "To you, God has made this all known; therefore, no one is as discerning and wise as you are. *You* shall be over my house, and all my people shall be ruled according to your word. Only in regard to the throne will I be greater than you."

None of the servants said anything. It was totally silent, and the environment seemed rather tense to me. Then, one of the officers started to speak, but the king interrupted him by calling in two officials. Next, he turned to me and said, "These men will take you to your new residence. I will talk with you later." The officials led me out while all the servants (the *other* servants, I should say now) remained with the king. I suspected that some heavy dialogues were going to take place among them.

The Ascent

My new residence was a very luxurious place. It was part of the complex of the court of Pharaoh and reminded me of Potiphar's house. It had a large reception area, and several inner rooms, and even its own bathing room. I wondered what the other prisoners thought when they realized that I did not come back. After the officials left, I remained by myself for several hours before the king called me, which gave me time to meditate on this sudden radical change of conditions. Sometimes I had thought about how it would be to be out of prison again, but I had never really been able to form an image of how I would react. But now I knew.

I surprised myself by not reacting with more excitement. Should I not be extraordinarily happy? I could not explain to myself why I was not. Was it because it was still so unreal to me that it had not yet begun to affect my emotions? Or was it that deep inside, I felt like a deserter toward those who would miss my company and need my support? Or could it be that I was intimidated by the immense responsibility that lay ahead of me and that I feared I would fail to meet the king's expectations?

"O *YHWH*, my Elohim, here I am, and I do not know what to think or what to do. Is this really your plan and design for me? I must trust and believe that it is. How else could this possibly have happened? The cupbearer really was an angel sent by You, after all."

However, how could I be of any help in this situation? I did not have any training or experience in any of the tasks that were involved in this. I really did not understand what the king expected from me. His words sounded so overwhelming. "*You shall be over my house, and all my people shall be ruled according to your word.*" Was he not exaggerating? That seemed to go far beyond what I had envisioned when Elohim had given me the thought of setting a man over the land to collect and store up the food. Why would the king think that I knew anything about government affairs?

I knew that *YHWH* was with me, no doubt about that, but that did not make my fear go away. I hoped the king would call me soon and give me more detailed instructions about my duties—that he would explain to me what he had in mind concerning my responsibilities. "Maybe I can explain to him that I am not really prepared for such a high position," I thought. "Maybe he will ask me what I think, if I wish to accept this new task, and if I think I am capable of fulfilling it. I am only experienced in being a shepherd boy, a slave, and a prisoner. Well, I do have some experience in managing an estate, but still, I am nothing like the counselors he is used to working with, who are all learned in all the wisdom of the Egyptians.[3] Right now, he must be in a meeting with them, and they will surely advise him to choose a more experienced man. He may still change his mind and retract his decision, or at least lower the number of responsibilities he was thinking of charging me with. After all, it seemed that he took his decision a little bit on the spur of the moment, before hearing and considering any counsel."

Later that day, the king called me and talked with me alone. I do not think I can explain how I felt during that conversation. It went far beyond everything that I could have ever imagined. "See, I am setting you over the entire land of Egypt. I am giving you complete authority over my people. Nobody can even lift up his hand or foot without your consent, so to speak. Only I will be above you in authority."

"My king," I dared to reply, "I am very honored by your trust in me, but I must tell you that I really have no idea how to govern a nation. I have never been in any place of authority except for being a steward at Potiphar's homestead and…well…at the prison."

"Are you resisting me?"

"Oh no, my king, surely not! But I feel that I cannot be in authority over your country. I do not have the preparation and the capacity to command your people. You have such highly educated and well-trained men at your court. Your elders with their great wisdom and experience—how could I teach them? All your great men, your officers and rulers—how could I command them?"

It all seemed so strange to me. If he had only put me in charge of the food collection and conservation project, I would have understood. That was what this was all about, after all, and I could not deny that it was me to whom Elohim had given the revelation. Such a charge would surely have been overwhelming to me, but I could see myself trusting Elohim to give me the grace to execute that job. However, the king was no longer talking about the dream, the years of abundance and the famine. He was now talking about ruling his land and his people! How could it be that the king of Egypt was asking me, a man with practically no education or experience, and whom he had known for less than a single day, to govern his country? It hardly made sense to me, and I started getting the feeling that there were other issues involved—issues I was not aware of.

"Let me explain something to you," he answered. "There are other issues involved—things that you do not comprehend that you need to know and understand. I know very well that you have not been educated in our schools or trained in agriculture, food conservation, construction of storehouses, or administration of businesses—and even less in many other tasks that are involved in ruling a nation. But those are not the main challenges for the man who is going to lead our country in the years to come.

"Every man can be educated. Every man can be trained, and many men are smart enough to learn new and difficult tasks. However, the real challenge—the core of the issue—is a *heart issue*, not an intellectual one. The wisdom this man needs goes far beyond mere knowledge and understanding. The responsibility of leading our nation through the years to come, of directing the enterprise of saving our people from perishing, demands—above anything else—a man of wisdom that comes from above.[4] He needs to be a man of righteousness, integrity, loyalty, and honesty toward Egypt as a nation, and therefore to me as the head of this nation. He must be a man of genuine love, mercy, and sacrifice for the people of Egypt.

"I have only known you for a very short time, but based on what I have heard about you and what I have seen in you, I believe you are such a man. From the moment you told me that there was no wisdom in you but that God alone has wisdom, that only *He* can give wisdom, I knew that God was with you. I could see His Spirit in you. Therefore, I did not doubt for a moment that He was going to give you the answers we need—the understanding of the dreams and the wisdom to respond to them. I can see that you are a man of wisdom from above, a man of righteousness, integrity, loyalty, and honesty—a man who knows, fears, and loves God. I did not choose you because of your capacity to rule or to execute the tasks that are involved. I chose you because I know that you are loyal—because of your character."

I understood that it was of no use to try further arguments and that the new order was a fact. However, I still had a thousand doubts and questions, even fears, in my heart and mind. Just think of what a radical, far-reaching decision it was for the king to set a Hebrew slave and prisoner over such a great and reputable nation as Egypt and to appoint him as a master over his wise men…as a ruler over his chiefs!

"My king, I do not want to oppose you in any way, but I beg you to give ear to my words and hear the concerns of my heart. What about all your great men—your counselors, your elders, your wise men, your rulers, your officers, your chiefs? How can I be in authority over them?" The king was silent for what seemed like a long time to me. I saw that he was thinking about giving me an answer. I knew that the reason why he thought so long was not that he did not know the answer, but that he was not sure how to explain it and how open he could or should be with me at this point.

Finally, he started talking. "Authority…authority is based on loyalty. If I am not loyal to God, what ground do I have to exercise authority over His people? On the other hand, I also totally depend on the loyalty of those under my authority. If they are not loyal to me, how can I be their king? Either I cease being their king, which will cause Egypt to decay into anarchy, or I must make them submit by force and power, which will cause the kingdom to turn into a tyranny. You need to know, and you will surely discover this during the time to come, that many of the elders and chiefs lack loyalty. They were already great men under my father's reign, and they have known me as a child. For me to govern this nation, I depend very much on their wisdom—their knowledge and understanding. They have much more experience than I have, and I do not doubt that they have the capacity to organize and oversee all the tasks involved in the collection and distribution of grain. However, they also have the capacity to decide who they will prefer over whom and to take advantage of the needs of the people in order to obtain great personal benefits. I need their capacity, but without loyalty, capacity becomes a deadly weapon."

I had never thought of the kingdom of Egypt in this way. Because of the way I had heard Potiphar talking about Pharaoh, I had always been under the impression that the king had absolute power over everyone under his authority.

When I expressed these thoughts to the king, he responded, "That is what most people think. However, when you were a child, did your father have absolute control over your and your brothers' behavior? Or did he depend on your loyalty? When you served Potiphar, was he in absolute control over the behavior of all his slaves? Or did he depend on your loyalty? In the kingdom, it is not different. In order to govern my people, I depend on their loyalty.

"Now, I do not want you to think that they are all evil. Under my father's rule, they served him with integrity, and men like Potiphar and some others surely are loyal to me. Nevertheless, many times, I feel weak, though I am the anointed king, and these men are often too hard and too strong for me.[5] I believe you can help me.

"Today, they have witnessed that you have superior wisdom, wisdom from above. They cannot but acknowledge that the Spirit of God is in you. Therefore, they cannot but humble themselves and bow their knees before you.[6] Therefore, today I give you authority over them and over all I have—all that is under my care. I give you authority over all my great men. Instruct and teach my elders and wise men according to your wisdom. Command my rulers and officers, control and discipline them, even bind them, according to your consideration, as you see fit.[7] I believe God has sent you to me to be a blessing to me and to my kingdom—to restore the order and the honor and glory of Egypt."

That night, I could hardly sleep. No, this time there were no chains and no cold, smelly night air. This time, thousands of thoughts ran through my mind. I tried to recall every word the king had spoken. As I tried to discern his underlying reasons and motives, I came to the conclusion that the deepest desire of his heart, if he could ask for anything he wanted, was to have a father who could help, teach, comfort, and strengthen him—someone whom he could trust, ask, and learn from. And when I started asking *YHWH* to bless him and to bless me and use me to be a true blessing to him, the strangest feeling came over me—that more than anything else, He wanted to establish me as a father to the king.[8]

Ruler over Egypt

The following days were very busy days to confirm and publicize the new order in the kingdom of Egypt. In the presence of all his servants and officers, as a sign of the absoluteness of this new status, the king solemnly took the ring from his hand and put it on my hand. This meant that every word from my mouth, any order that I gave, any decision that I took, was beforehand supported and confirmed by the king himself.

After that, several public ceremonies followed to present me to the people of Egypt as lord of the land. Pharaoh presented me with an Egyptian name that he had chosen for me. I understood very well that he found it unfit for me to use my Hebrew name in this office, and it did not offend me. I did not feel that my own name, the one that bears the name of *YHWH*, my Elohim, was taken away from me. I have never ceased to use that name, and I plan to continue using it till the end of my life. Even the king himself would call me by that name sometimes.[9] Therefore, I did not feel that my name had changed, but rather that a new name was added unto me, symbolizing the inauguration of a new season in my life, a new reality. I had now become part of Egypt, and the people of Egypt were my people now. As a crown and seal on that new reality, the king chose a woman for me to be my helpmeet in this new life.

More than ever, I was totally convinced that I had been brought to this land and kept here by the hand of *YHWH*, the Elohim of the heavens, and that it was His will for me that I leave behind my past and my roots. I hope you understand me well. I am not saying that I in any way felt I had ceased to be a part of the chosen nation of Abraham, Isaac, and Israel. But I understood that *YHWH* wanted me to give my life for Egypt without limitations. Therefore, in a sense and at least for a season, it was necessary for Him to make me *forget* my past and even the house of my father.[10] This was the only way that I could fulfill His calling and purpose in this land and bear the fruit that He had destined for me to produce.

It may seem strange to you that I never took it on me to travel to Canaan to see my father or at least to somehow let him know that I was alive and well. But I hope you can see that it was in obedience to the direction that *YHWH* gave me to follow. Maybe one day He would guide me to see my father and brothers again, but I left that in His hand. My duty was to consecrate my life to the responsibilities that He had charged me with. You see, I was still learning that only if I trusted Him and obeyed His word—only if I were His faithful and loyal slave—could the Blessing of Abraham become a reality in my life.

In the beginning, my time as lord of the land was not easy. The challenges with the counselors, rulers, high officers, and elders and with their attitudes toward me—it was all just as I had expected. They obeyed me as was required, but the situation was often stressful, and it reminded me of the time when Potiphar had put me over his household and stewards. There were times when they were very uncooperative, as if they rejoiced in my failures. Many times I talked with them, individually or as a team, and I shared with them that I could not fulfill my tasks without their help, counsel, wisdom, and experience. And little by little, I succeeded in winning their confidence, respect, and loyalty. However, there were some who could not so easily forget that I was "just a Hebrew," and I found it very difficult to know how to respond to that. Should I use force and control them, even "bind" them, as the king had authorized me to do? Or should I try to keep peace and overlook their shortcomings? In those times, I realized how true the words of the king had been when he said that authority always depends on loyalty and that without loyalty it will turn into either tyranny or anarchy.

Eventually, as the years passed, all their resistance disappeared. Today, so many years later, I can truly say that I am experiencing the full support and respect of all the servants of the king.

The first thing I did after taking office was to travel the land. I had hardly ever left Potiphar's house and knew very little of the country. Next, I commissioned local officers in each city who would oversee the construction of storehouses and start the collection of the grain from their corresponding provinces. Each local officer kept records of the quantities they were storing, and I processed all the data in my office. I put a steward in charge of the daily work at my office; he worked closely with me and managed the office whenever I had to travel. His position was very similar to mine at Potiphar's house, where I had been in charge of the daily work and had managed the homestead when my master needed to leave.

During the first years, I needed to keep strict supervision over establishing, confirming, and sometimes adjusting the regulations on which the collection of the grain was based. In the following years, I delegated much of the dealing with the farmers to the local officers. I did not pay for the grain; I did not buy it. There was no budget for that. Instead, I charged it as tax. The amount that Elohim had put in my mind from the beginning was one-fifth, twenty parts per every hundred parts. One-fifth seemed to me a righteous and reasonable amount for each citizen to contribute to the needs of the country. Very soon, however, I discovered that the officers had great difficulties collecting the duties.

It appeared that many people had no sense of duty at all for the support of their king and their nation, and my officers started experiencing exactly the same lack of loyalty from the citizens as they themselves had expressed toward the king and, in a lesser measure, toward me! I came to realize that the lack of loyalty was not just a problem in the circles of elders and rulers; it was all through the nation, at every level. I often discussed these issues with my officers and counselors. How do we respond to those who are unwilling to obey the regulations? Do we have to use force? Do we accept that parts of the nation do not participate?

"Tell the people that this nation needs their loyalty," I told my officers. "Teach them that lack of loyalty will lead either to anarchy or to tyranny." These words of the king were so true, and it became increasingly clear to me what he had meant when he talked about restoring the order and the honor and glory of Egypt.

Despite the many challenges we faced, my officers did a great work to reach the goal of collecting the quantities we had estimated necessary for the survival of the nation. We also took into consideration that the surrounding nations were not preparing for the famine at all and that most likely, people from there would come and ask us to sell to them as well. Toward the end of the seven good years, the crops became so abundant, and the provision in each city was so beyond measure, that we had no way of keeping the records and registering the amounts. There were no numbers that would adequately represent the actual stockpile.

Then, at the end of seven years, the world changed.

That next year, many farmers still planted grain, hoping that maybe the rumors were not true, but their fields produced very little. The seemingly eternal water flow of the great Nile River began to diminish and reached the lowest level the older people had ever witnessed. The following years, the situation became increasingly grievous.

The water level continued to decrease. Eventually, some of the branches and many of the artificial canals became totally dry, showing large cracks. Although there was always enough water for people and cattle to drink, it was no longer enough to grow any crops. I think you know that we irrigate our fields, so our agriculture does not depend so much on rain—I mean, not local rain; it depends on rain in the countries higher up from us where the Great River comes from. We use the river water to feed extensive irrigation systems. But at that time, just watching the former mighty river turning green from algae and the impressive network of branches and canals being transformed into mud puddles—it just made me cry.

The King's Court

The first year of the drought, and to a certain extent also the second and even part of the third year, many people still could survive or partly sustain themselves from what they had stocked up in their homes, the small amounts of grain that their land still produced, their fruit trees, and their cattle. Through those entire seven years, some grass always grew, especially in the lower parts of the country. In the later years of the famine, this pastureland was hardly enough for cattle and horses anymore, but sheep and goats could still be maintained. However, most people did not have sheep or goats; our people prefer keeping cattle.

Gradually, more and more parts of the country became famished, and in their need, the people came to the king and cried out for help. The king talked with them and told them to come to me. He said that I was in charge of the food aid program and that I would instruct them in what to do. Then, when they came to me, I sent them to the officers who were in charge of the storehouses in each city. I ordered the officers to open the storehouses and to start distributing the food according to the regulations that we had established. We had determined fair prices for the food and made sure that the grain was only sold depending on the actual needs of each household.

Every citizen needed to be registered correctly in order to have the right to buy, but also to prevent him from buying in multiple cities. We exercised strict control to avoid any conditions that could give room for a black market or fraud. Very often, I realized how certain the words of the king were when he had said that the main challenge of leading our country through these years of trouble would be in the area of righteousness and integrity!

I was personally taking care of the main storage at my office, from which I supplied the house of the king, including his servants and the priests, who, because of their office, were always provided for by the king. Besides that, I also took care of those who, for one reason or another, did not belong to any of the cities, especially the people from neighboring countries.

Just as we had expected, in the beginning we were selling more grain to foreigners than to our own people. In our land, practically everybody had heard about the famine that was coming, and although maybe not everybody believed it, it had caused most people to stock food. In addition, it was well known from history that Egypt was the land to go to in times of famine. Because of our irrigation systems, during seasons of drought, we can handle the situation much longer than, for example, the land of Canaan. That country, even though it is good land, totally depends on regular rain from heaven, from the beginning of the year to the end.[11] So, as early as in the second year of the famine, people from the surrounding lands started coming for food.

Chapter 5
Visitors from Canaan

Arrival of the Shepherds

"Some shepherds from Canaan are here to buy grain."

"Let them come in."

My steward let them in and brought them forward. When they came closer, I could not believe what I saw.

"No, this cannot be true!" I thought. "Are they really here? Yes, no doubt they are!" They did not speak a word. They looked very intimidated by the environment, and when they had come close to me, they bowed down deeply, touching the floor with their foreheads. That moment, I remembered my dream.[1] I had forgotten about it, Elohim had made me forget about it, but now, as I saw it fulfilled before my eyes, I remembered it. This was what I had seen in my dream!

I recognized all of them, even though they were twenty-two years older than when I had last seen them. Reuben, Simeon, Levi, Judah...all of them were here. All of them? All of them...but Benjamin.

What would I do? Would I reveal my identity? For a moment, I felt great joy in my heart and desired to hug them and let them know that all was well, that I had wholeheartedly forgiven them, and that I knew that it had all been the design of *YHWH* that I was here. But then, when I realized that Benjamin, my little brother, was not with them, a wave of fear came over me. Why had Benjamin not come with them? What had happened to him? Had Father made him the heir, once he had lost hope that I would return and Benjamin had become my mother's oldest son? Had my brothers, therefore, done something to him as well? Had they sold him, or maybe worse? And what had happened with Father? Was he still alive, maybe consumed by sorrow? Or had he descended into the grave in mourning? I needed to know. I would not reveal who I was until I knew what had happened.

How would I work this out? While they were bowing down, rising up, and waiting for me to speak, my mind worked on forming a strategy. I fixed my eyes on them and looked at each of their faces, still processing my thoughts. Then I turned to my interpreter and said, "Ask them who they are and where they have come from."

They trembled with fear as they noticed my severity. I asked many questions about their families and their personal lives and occupations, as if I were verifying whether there were any contradictions in their stories. That made them feel that I mistrusted them, which made them even more fearful. They did not dare look at me; they felt less uncomfortable looking at my interpreter.

The conversation went on for a long time. I discovered that my father and brother were still alive. They also mentioned their *other brother*. They did not say that they had sold him; they just said that he was no more. Therefore, I understood that they did not expect me to have been able to survive the way they thought I had been treated.

The fact that Benjamin was still alive gave me some relief, but it was far from satisfying. What could be the reason that he had not come with them? Did they hate him? Did Father not trust them and fear that they would do something to him once they were out of his sight? Or could it be that they had changed and accepted Benjamin, and they had just left him at home to take care of Father? Could it be that seeing the suffering of their father had caused them pain and sorrow and that it had led them to repentance? Could it be that watching him mourning for me had softened their hearts? Or were they just waiting until Father died, planning to kill or sell Benjamin then? Or, not wanting to carry the load of their guilt, were they instead waiting for an opportunity to get rid of their brother in a way in which they could wash their hands in innocence?

"I need to see my brother and watch how they treat him," I thought. "Somehow, I must make him come to me."

After a long time of interrogation, I concluded, "You are liars. You have not come to buy grain. You are taking advantage of our goodness and mercy toward the nations, as we have opened our borders for many people in need to come and buy food. Surely you are spies who have come to discover the weaker parts of our land." I could feel the eyes of my steward on me even without watching him, and I could see the confusion in the eyes of my interpreter. They had never seen me this way before, and they were surely questioning why I was acting like this. "I do not believe you," I continued. "If you had another brother, then he would also have come with you. If he were here, I would believe you, but now, your story is not believable. You are spies. I tell you what we will do. You will stay here in prison. One of you may leave, and if he comes back with your other brother, then your words will be confirmed. If not, that will be proof that you are liars, and you will be judged before Pharaoh." Then I called the officers and told them to put them all in prison.

After everybody had gone, my steward came to me. "My lord, why do you believe these men are spies?"

"They are not spies," I replied, "these men are shepherds from Canaan."

"I do not understand you. Why are you treating them this way? They are frightened. I have never seen you treat anybody like this!"

I looked at him and said, "They are my brothers."

"Your brothers? The ones you told me about, who sold you as a slave?"

"Yes, they are the ones who sold me."

"You are still angry with them, right? Are you taking revenge? I thought that you had forgiven them. Did you not tell us that you believed that *YHWH*, your God, had brought you here, that He was powerful to use evil for good? Did you not teach all of us that we were not to judge but to forgive our enemies, even if they had done the worst to us, and that we must always seek to be a blessing to them?"

"Believe me," I replied, "I have forgiven them. I am not angry with them. I love them."

"My lord, sometimes you are hard to understand. Many times, you have taught us things that I, and most of us, did not immediately understand. Sometimes we even disagreed with you. But as you continued explaining, almost all of us could see that you were always right. However, this time, with all due respect, I cannot see how this can be right. I believe that if you have really forgiven them, you must treat them differently."

"Listen. Let me explain to you why I am doing what I am doing."

I told him many things that I had never told him before—about my childhood, the wives of my father, the way he had preferred my mother over his other wives, the way he had preferred me over my older brothers, how my brothers used to treat and deceive my father, and many other things. I told him about my fear, fear of how they might be treating my father now and what they would do to my little brother. I told him how God had made me forget about all those fears and how He had taught me to trust Him to take care of the things that He had not given me the responsibility for, even my father and my brothers. But now, God Himself had brought my brothers back to me, and therefore, I understood that He was giving me the responsibility for them.

"During all these years after I left them, I have learned so much about *YHWH*, the God of our fathers—so many things that they do not know or understand. And it is my responsibility now to feed them, both body and soul. I must accept the responsibility that *YHWH* is giving me. I cannot just send them away and let them continue in their ways."

"So what is your plan?"

"We will keep them here a few days. Then we will send the oldest to Canaan, and we will wait until he comes back with my youngest brother. Meanwhile, the others will remain here in prison."

"I think you should not send one by himself; that is too dangerous. I think you should send at least two or three. Or why do we not keep just one and let all the others go? They would surely come back, even if we kept just one of them here, do you not think so? Must we not also think of their families? Their wives and children are in need of the provision that they came to buy."

"You may be right. I will think about it. However, you need to keep something in mind. You feel sorry for them because you have seen the fear in their eyes. But that fear does not make them righteous. The people who fear them are many more than those whom they fear. Be not led by emotions when *YHWH* gives you the responsibility to rule. You must teach, instruct, correct, rebuke, and even punish in the name of *YHWH* according to righteousness and truth, not according to your emotions, just like a shepherd uses a rod and a staff to correct and comfort the sheep he cares for.[2] At times that may seem merciless, even cruel. But in the end, it brings healing to their souls.

"This is the way in which *YHWH* corrects, as a loving father who does not withhold the rod. That is the road where *YHWH* has led me—a road of suffering, but a road that has led me to become who I am today. I would not trade the experience of walking this road for all the gold in the world, no matter how hard it often was, and I will not withhold this experience from others whom *YHWH* puts under my care, no matter how loudly my emotions protest."

That night, I kept thinking about my brothers for a long time. All of a sudden, they were back in my life. *YHWH* had led me to forget about my dreams a long time ago, and it was also *YHWH* who had made me remember my dreams. *YHWH* had made me forget those in my father's house, and this day He Himself had brought them back to me. I had never sent for them; they had come by themselves, by the hand of *YHWH*. And when they came, I did not tell them to bow down so that the dream would be fulfilled—they bowed by their own will, by the hand of *YHWH*. It was *YHWH* Himself who fulfilled the dream!

More than ever, I realized that I would never have been able to fulfill the dreams by my own wisdom and strength.

"O Elohim, how thankful I am that You made me forget my dreams and that You kept me from running after their fulfillment. How many errors I would have made! How many others would I have hurt, not even considering that they also might have their dreams?

Even if I had succeeded in accomplishing many goals, I would still not have reached nor even understood what You had for me. What was my understanding of the dreams at the time that You gave them to me? '*Do you really think that you will rule and reign over us?*' my brothers had said. That was what they thought it meant, and honestly, I thought they could be right.

"But this day, I saw the fulfillment of that dream before my eyes, and behold, I was not ruling over them at all! Did their action of bowing down mean submission to my authority, or was it rather an expression of dependency and respect? The fact that it was *me* to whom they bowed down, did that mean that I was in a position to exercise power over them? Rather, it meant that I was appointed to care for them and feed them! Did the fact that they humbled themselves before me mean that they would serve me? It rather turned out that I was serving them!

"Oh, how often and how easily do we, as rulers of the nations, focus on our dreams, visions, and ambitions and seek to be served by those under our authority for the fulfillment of our own desires!

"O *YHWH*, my Elohim, you have protected me from fulfilling my dream according to my own interpretation, an interpretation based on my selfishness and pride. But Your thoughts are so different. You have brought me here, not to be served, but to serve. You have brought me here, not to fulfill my dreams, but to know and understand the dreams of those around me—to serve them for the satisfaction of *their* needs and the fulfillment of *their* desires."

And what about the other dream? I told you that I had had two dreams, right? The first one with the sheaves and the other one about the sun, moon, and eleven stars. Would my father come and bow down before me, if he was indeed the one represented by the sun? Would Benjamin come to complete the number eleven? And who would be the moon?

I must say that, even until today, I have never been completely sure about the meaning of that dream. But looking back on how the story has unfolded, I often think that the sun rather represented Pharaoh, and the moon and stars the great men and the people of Egypt. It may be true that Pharaoh never bowed down for me. But the day I gave him the interpretation of his dreams, I could see an attitude of deep respect toward me, and he probably would have bowed down if I had been alone with him—not to adore me, but humbling himself before the Spirit of Elohim, whom he saw was in me, according to his own words.[3]

Whatever the precise meaning is, the question remains of why Elohim had given me the dreams. If I could and should not do anything to fulfill them, and if He even wanted me to forget them, what then was the purpose of the dreams? I will tell you what I think about that, based on what I personally experienced.

If I had not had the dream, I think that I would not have discerned the transcendental significance of the event. I would just have focused on the natural and obvious reason for my brothers' visit—I would have sold them the grain, and that would have been it. Because of the dream, I understood that Elohim had a greater purpose. If Elohim had planned and ordained this to happen, then He must have very special reasons; and if He had already shown this to me so many years before then He must be giving me a special task, a special mission, a special responsibility.

Therefore, at the very moment when Elohim fulfilled the dream before my eyes I knew that Elohim was giving me a responsibility for my brothers that went far beyond providing food for their bodies. I understood that Elohim was putting them under my care. He was putting them in "my household" and therefore giving me the responsibility for providing them with food for body and soul in due season.[4] I knew that I not only had to feed them and their families with grain, but that I must also feed them spiritually, discerning the condition of their hearts. I was to lead, guide, and correct them according to righteousness and truth, on the road to humility, repentance, forgiveness, reconciliation, and restoration. You see, the purpose of the dream was not that I should run after its fulfillment. Rather, once I had seen the fulfillment of the dream before my eyes, it helped and served me to recognize and understand the mission and responsibility that Elohim was giving me.

On the third day of their captivity, I went to see my brothers. They were afraid to see me, but at the same time, they had some hope that I would make a decision that was favorable to them. "I am a God-fearing man," I said. "I know that your families are in need of food and are waiting for you to come back. This is what we will do so that you and your families may live. One of you will stay here in prison; the rest of you may go back now and take the provision to your families. Once you come back with your younger brother, then your words will be confirmed, and your brother who remains here will be released to you."

In their desperation, they tried to understand why all this adversity was coming over them. They thought, of course, that I did not understand anything they said as they talked among themselves. It surprised me that they did not curse me or the people of Egypt, blaming me or us for being irrational and cruel. Instead, they took the guilt upon themselves and believed that this was the consequence of their own mischief. They talked about how they had treated me and sold me. They remembered seeing how desperate I was and how cruel they had been by not caring about that at all. From Reuben's words, I understood that he had not been in agreement with the others about selling me. "I told you not to harm the boy, but you did not listen to me," he said.

When I heard them talking about me, and watched how their feelings of guilt caused this affliction that, after twenty-two years, was still persecuting them, I could no longer control myself, and I had to turn away from them. I hurried into an inner room where I cried: I cried because I could see the pain they lived with, but also for joy, seeing that Elohim was indeed using me to lead them to humility, acknowledgment of their evil, and repentance. Then I washed my face and returned to them, acting as if I had had to attend to other business. Only my steward knew better and noticed the expression on my face.

"Are your emotions protesting?" he whispered.

"You know me too well," I said. Then I turned back to my brothers.

I chose Simeon, the second oldest, to stay. I knew that Father had given Reuben, the oldest, the responsibility for the journey, and I wanted to respect that. I told my steward to make sure to give them provisions for the way, besides the amount of grain that they had come to buy and had paid for. I also told him to put all the money back in their sacks. From the many details that they had told me during the interrogation, I knew that their wealth had greatly decreased since the famine began. They still had herds and flocks, but they were not nearly as large as they used to be. They had no camels anymore; they had come all the way with donkeys.

After they left, my normal daily responsibilities continued. Every day, I asked my steward how Simeon was doing. He was being treated well by the officer in charge, but he had to remain in prison. When after a number of weeks none of my other brothers had returned, I started to get worried. They should have been back by now. What could be going on? Were they afraid to come back? Would Father not allow Benjamin to leave him? Was he afraid to lose him as well, and considered it better to lose Simeon than to lose Benjamin? Should I have kept nine of them here, as my original plan was? Had I been too soft, allowing my emotions to influence, or even dominate, my decisions?

Many more weeks went by, and I realized that either Simeon was just not important enough to my other brothers to risk their lives or freedom, or he was not important enough to Father to risk Benjamin. My only hope was that they would have to come back once they ran out of food for their families.

Benjamin

What a joy I felt the day my brothers returned—especially when I saw that Benjamin was with them! It was very hard for me to meet them without being overwhelmed by emotions. I told my steward to receive them and to take them to my residence so that they could rest and wash up while some of the servants took care of the donkeys. "Tell them that I will talk with them later."

They acted very nervous; I think that they suspected they were going to be taken to prison again. They apologized to my steward about the money that they had found in their bags. They had really not stolen it, and they had no idea how it got there, they explained. My steward told them not to worry—that he had received the money and that he would not accept it back from them. They should thank God, he said. "Your God, the God of your father, has given you the money."

That was not a lie; I had been acting in the name of *YHWH*.

They also showed him some gifts from Canaan that Father had sent for me. While they waited for me, my steward told the officers to bring Simeon out, which made them more relaxed. That, and the fact that Benjamin was with them, who could confirm every word they had said, gave them hope that maybe everything would go well now.

Around noon, I went to my house to join them. I greeted them kindly but could not allow myself to be too familiar. They bowed down before me and gave me the gift they had brought. "This is a gift from your servant, our father." Father had sent some balm, spices, and different kinds of nuts. It seemed that at least some trees were still producing fruit, despite the drought. I thanked them and asked how their father was doing.

Then the great moment arrived. "Is this your youngest brother, of whom you spoke to me?" When I looked at him and saw his face, I was deeply moved with a mixture of emotions. There was intense joy on seeing him again, but on the other hand, I also had great worries about his future, about what might hang over his head. When I saw him standing there surrounded by my brothers, I remembered my own childhood, the fears I had always lived with.

"May God have mercy on you, my son," I said, trying to give my voice a fatherly or elderly sound. But then I could not restrain my emotions any longer. I hurried to my chamber and wept. So many memories of my childhood went through my mind: the time when Benjamin was born, and how he and I had grown up together without a mother. He had become a strong young man now, but to me, he would forever be my little brother. Just as all my other brothers did, he had his own family now as well. But my father, as the patriarch, ruled over all of them as the chief of the tribe—the tribe of the Hebrews.

"Be strong now! You are not finished yet," I told myself, as I returned from my chamber.

"Serve the food," I ordered my servants. They had prepared an abundant dinner and treated my brothers as honored guests. I wish you could have seen the astonishment in their faces when they were assigned places in the order of their births, just as I had instructed my steward to do! According to protocol, I did not sit down with them; I ate with my own servants. During the entire time, I was watching them and trying to discern how they treated Benjamin. I told my servants to honor him especially by serving him the best and most abundant portions, just to see how my brothers would react to seeing their youngest brother being preferred and spoiled.

The time we spent eating was pleasant, and I did not get the impression in any way that Benjamin was uncomfortable in the company of his brothers. They treated one another in a friendly manner, and I could not discern any envy or friction. The whole afternoon became just a merry celebration. I could see that they were very relieved by the manner in which they were being treated. I overheard them talking about Father, how they could not wait to tell him about everything that had happened to them and how different this trip had been from the first. It was a joy to see how well all my brothers got along with one another and how kindly they related to Benjamin.

My plan had been to make myself known to them at the climax of the feast, but as it continued, doubt crept into my mind. Was I convinced too soon? Was the way they treated one another, and especially Benjamin, their normal behavior, or were they so excited and in such a good and friendly mood because of the relief from their fear? Would their true characters reveal themselves as soon as they returned to their normal lives?

The feast came to an end, and my brothers went to the inn where they were to spend the night. "Come back early tomorrow to receive the grain, and as soon as the sun comes up, I will send you away." I had never seen such happiness in their faces, and I felt almost like a cruel man as I thought of bringing one more test to their lives. But I was committed to not being led by my emotions. "My Elohim, I know that You have given me a responsibility, and I will fulfill that to the end in Your name."

My steward approached me. I could see that he was once again confused by my actions. "I thought that you were going to make yourself known to them during the feast."

"So did I. But it is not the time yet. Come to see me early tomorrow, before dawn, and then I will let you know what we will do. I need to talk with *YHWH* first." Then I retreated to my chambers to pray.

"O *YHWH*, Elohim of my fathers, I am so thankful that You have allowed me to see my little brother again. I am so happy to see that my brothers seem to love him. Nevertheless, I cannot wash away that doubt from my mind. How will it be when they are back in Canaan? How will it be once You take Father home? What must I do to try them and to reveal the intentions of their hearts? What must I do to help them to further acknowledge their faults and lead them on this road of repentance, forgiveness, reconciliation, and restoration? Speak to me. Give me Your wisdom, and make me understand Your ways."

My steward came to my office very early. I could see that he had a sincere interest in the well-being of my brothers. Although he did not want to show it, I knew that it was hard for him to watch the way I treated them.

"Do you have a plan?"

"Yes. I am not sure if you are going to like it, but I need your full cooperation."

"You can count on me."

"Well, then. I want you to know that I still have doubts. What it comes down to is that I am not sure if my brothers have accepted Benjamin wholeheartedly. Maybe they have just given up, not seeing an opportunity to get rid of him. Maybe they have just accepted him and my father's special love for him because they have no choice. The only way to know what is in their hearts is by giving them the opportunity to get Benjamin out of their way in such a manner that they are innocent and cannot be blamed.

"So this is what we are going to do. We are going to arrest Benjamin and put him in prison or make him a slave. Then we will send the rest of them back to Canaan."

"And what are we going to accuse him of?"

"Stealing. When the servants fill their sacks, you will put their money back with the grain, and then you will put my silver cup on top of that in Benjamin's sack.

Make sure that nobody sees it, not even the servants. Then, when they get on their way, as soon as they are outside the city, take a few of the officers with you and follow them. When you overtake them, say, 'What have you done? Why have you returned evil for good? How could you take the cup from which my lord drinks?'"

"Oh, my lord, I do not know if I can do this."

"You must! Next, let the officers search the sacks, and when they find the cup, you tell them that you will take Benjamin back and that all others must leave Egypt and return to Canaan."

"What are you going to do with Benjamin then?"

"I do not know yet. It is my hope that it will not go that far. If my brothers really have changed, then they will not abandon Benjamin. At least one of them will follow you and come back with him. However, if they envy him deep in their hearts and wish that he were out of their lives, they will return to Canaan and say to their father, 'Benjamin was taken by force by security officers in Egypt, and we were sent out of the country. There was nothing we could do.' Then they can go the rest of their lives without ever feeling guilty. This will be their golden opportunity."

He did not answer me; he just stared at the ground.

"Make haste now! Go and tell the servants to fill the sacks. Here, take my cup. And do not forget the money."

It was still before sunrise when the small caravan left. We waited long enough to give them time to leave the city and get to the road toward Canaan. Then I gave the sign for my steward to start the pursuit. That whole time until my steward returned, I felt greatly strained. How would my brothers react? How would this end? I tried to imagine all the possible scenarios and checked off the ones that were least likely. I calculated how much time it would take for my steward and the officers to return. Reaching them would not take very long; our horses were much faster than their heavily loaded donkeys. Next would come rebuking my brothers, unloading and searching all the sacks, and then the arrest of Benjamin. The way back would be slower, no faster than Benjamin could walk.

Once I thought that enough time had passed and that they should be on their way back, I kept looking out my window to see if they were coming yet. Why was it taking so long? How had they responded? Had they continued on their way to Canaan, according to the command of my steward? Had they abandoned Benjamin? Oh, how much I desired that they had begged the steward to give them permission to support their younger brother and that at least one or maybe two of them would come back with him! "Oh, let it be so! Please, my Elohim, let it be."

Then I saw my steward's chariot appearing. After him came the chariot of the first officer with Benjamin walking behind him, his hands tied to the chariot. Next in the procession were the other officers. I do not remember ever in my life having felt my heart pounding more strongly than at that moment. Would one of my brothers follow?

Then I saw one of them walking behind the officers along with his donkey, although I could not see from that distance which of them it was. Then came another one! And then another! All of them had come back!

I went into my chamber, and I think that I wept more intensely than ever before, even more than in my worst times of despair. I allowed my emotions to take control of me while I awaited my steward's arrival, under the condition that they would be back under my control when it was time to finish my responsibility. When they arrived at my office, I was fully back in my role as the harsh lord of the land.

They came to me and fell down before me. When I saw their faces, I could see that their eyes were full of anguish and that they were without any hope that this could end well for them.

"What is this that you have done? Can you not understand that a man like me knows how to practice divination? Did you really think that I would not find out immediately, before you had a chance to escape the country?"

My brother Judah took the lead and spoke on behalf of all. "My lord, there is nothing we can say. Our God has found iniquity in your servants. He is judging us for the evil we have done. We accept His punishment. Here we are; take us as your slaves, all of us."

"I would never do such a thing. I am a righteous man. Far be it from me to condemn and punish innocent people. Only the man in whose power the cup was found will be declared guilty. He will stay here and be my slave. The rest of you go up in peace to your father."

Then Judah came forward and bowed down deeply before me. "My lord, please allow me to speak one word before you take our brother and before you send us away. When you asked us if we had a father and other brothers, we told you that we had indeed another brother, much younger and from a different mother than the rest of us. He had an older brother from the same mother, but he has died.

"Our father loves our youngest brother very much, and he is always fearful that something may happen to him. When we told our father that he had to let him come with us to Egypt, he told us, 'No, Benjamin cannot go. You know very well that my wife bore me only two sons, and one of them has been torn in pieces by wild animals; if something also happens to my other son, I will descend with sorrow into the grave.' Then I told my father that I would respond to him for his son and that the guilt would be upon me if something happened to him. So now, my lord, we cannot go home to my father without his son. I cannot bear to watch the suffering this will bring to my father all the days of the rest of his life. Therefore, my lord, I beg you to take me instead of my younger brother. Take me as your slave, but let my brother return to his father."

My eyes were filled with tears, and I could no longer restrain myself. *"We cannot go home to my father without his son,"* Judah had said. Would they not go home without his son anyway? Was he himself not a son, just as well as Benjamin? How could he have come to humble himself so deeply as to accept without reproach or bitterness that he was of so little value to his father, hardly considered a son, other than by the hand and Spirit of *YHWH*? Now I knew that *YHWH* had not only changed my life by leading me through deserts and valleys of the shadow of death, but His hand had also transformed them!

My heart could no longer contain the joy I felt. I cried out to everybody who was with me and told all of them to leave, including my interpreter, and when I was left alone with my brothers, I wept and cried so loudly that everybody at the court could hear me.

"I am Joseph! Is my father still alive?"

First, they did not know what to do. They were so confused; this was not real to them.

Again I said, "I am Joseph—your brother, Joseph, the one you sold to Egypt. Be not afraid; everything is well. I am not angry with you; I know that it was the hand of *YHWH*, the Elohim of our fathers, who has brought me here. He has used all evil for good."

They were still confused. In part, they could not believe what I said, and as far as they did believe it, it caused them more fear than joy.

After I had given them some time to recover from their fright and astonishment, we went to meet in my house. It became a very emotional time. Without the need to restrain myself any longer, I hugged Benjamin for a long time, and after him, also all my other brothers. Once we sat down, we talked about many things. It was strange to hear myself talking in Hebrew again after so many years.

First of all, I reassured them that all was well with me, that I had no feelings of hurt or anger against them, and that *YHWH*, our Elohim, had turned all evil into good. I also wanted to hear more stories and details about everything that had happened with them during all these years, especially about how Father was doing. They told me how hard it had been these last two years because of the drought.

Then I told them about the vision that Elohim had given to Pharaoh. "Almost ten years ago, Pharaoh had a dream from Elohim. He did not know what it meant, but another of his servants told him about me because I had interpreted a dream for him years earlier. It is a very long story, but the main thing is that Elohim showed me the meaning of Pharaoh's dream, and it revealed seven prosperous years followed by seven years of famine. Because Pharaoh could see that Elohim was with me, he set me over the entire land of Egypt.

"Now he lets me make almost all the important decisions, and in the few cases when he does make a decision, he will not do so without asking my advice first. I often feel that Elohim has established me as a father to him."[5] I shared that the king had given me the responsibility of developing and overseeing the food distribution program that we had, to save the lives of the people of Egypt and the surrounding nations.

When I mentioned that there were still five years of famine to come, I could see the worry in their faces.

Reuben, the oldest, spoke up. "We have already lost the majority of our herds and flocks. How are we going to make it through this? The Canaanites have always tolerated us living among them, but how will it be now that the land is no longer enough even for themselves?"

"Well, El Shaddai has sent me before you, to preserve you a posterity in the land and to save your lives by a great deliverance. This is what you must do. Go to my father, and let him know that I am alive and well. Tell him that Elohim has made me lord of all of Egypt and that I want all of you to come here as soon as you can, with your families, your herds and your flocks, and all you still have. I will talk with Pharaoh, and he will surely be happy to let you live in the lowlands, in the land of Goshen, which is good pastureland. There I will provide for all of you so that you will not perish in poverty."

When Pharaoh heard that my brothers were in Egypt, he and all his servants were very pleased. "Tell them to bring their families and let them live in our land!" the king said. "You must send horses and chariots for their wives and children and especially for your father. When they come, we will give them the best of our land."

That night, I kept thinking about everything my brothers, and especially Judah, had said. Surely my Elohim is also their Elohim! Judah had told me how *YHWH* had led him on a long road of hardships, which had broken the old, merciless Judah whom I had known. He would never be able to see Father lose another son whom he loved. "I know what it means to lose two sons," he told me. "I lost two of my sons.[6] I wish nobody this suffering, but I must admit that I deserved it. Elohim has used it to transform me, and it has helped me to become the man I am today...although it was not until my daughter-in-law confronted me with my iniquity and hypocrisy that I finally humbled myself."[7]

Very early that next morning, I sent them away, together with several officers who drove the chariots. I also gave them provision for the journey and gifts for their families, according to the orders of the king.

Reunited

Several weeks passed before the day Judah arrived at my office. Father had sent him ahead to let me know that the whole family had come to the land of Goshen. As soon as he arrived, I went down with him to meet them there. Words do not exist to adequately express the feelings that came over me when I saw my father, nor could I find words to say to him. The only thing I could do was fall on his neck and weep.

Finally, he said, "Today, everything I have hoped for has been fulfilled. I have no other desires left, no other requests, no other blessings to ask for. Everything is well now; I can descend into the grave in peace."

Then I met all the others, my brothers' wives and children, about sixty persons altogether. My memories went back to the time when I was a little child, when we had traveled from Padan Aram to Canaan. It was quite a contrast. Really, not much was left from that glorious caravan made up of many servants and maids, hundreds of camels and donkeys for them and us to ride on, large herds of cattle, and flocks of innumerable sheep and goats.

It did not make me sad, though, and I did not charge *YHWH* with wrongdoing.[8] I knew that their humiliation and the loss of their wealth were not without purpose. "I have no doubt that it is You, *YHWH*, the Elohim of Abraham and the Elohim of Isaac, who for Your own sake—for Your own sake—are testing them in the furnace of affliction. As You have refined me and taught me to listen to You, to let You guide me without need for bits and bridles, so are You also refining them.[9] I know that all these things will work together for good according to Your eternal purposes.[10] You are El Shaddai, the Almighty, the First and the Last. Yours alone is the glory from the foundation of the earth until eternity."

I stayed with them for several days. There were so many things that I needed to talk about with Father. I shared with him how *YHWH* had led me through hardships, but also how it all had worked together for good. I told him how He had taught me the mysteries of the Blessing of Abraham—that I had learned that *YHWH* had chosen us to bless us in order that we would be a blessing to those around us.

"Elohim has been fulfilling the Blessing in my life all these years, as He has allowed me to be a blessing to those in the house of Potiphar and to many prisoners. And now, *YHWH* has established me as a father to Pharaoh in order to also be a blessing to the king and the entire nation of Egypt. Pharaoh has set me as a commander over his rulers and as a teacher over his elders, and I know that it is *YHWH* Himself who has chosen me for this, so that I may command and teach them to keep His way, to do righteousness and justice."[11]

When Father shared his story, he did not show any bitterness about the famine or the calamities that had come over them. "All is well with me. You are still alive, and El Shaddai has allowed me to see you again," he kept repeating. "I do not seek any other blessing.

"My son, all my life I have been seeking the blessings for myself. Surely, I must say that I have succeeded in achieving everything I was going after; I have become a man of great wealth, and you know that. Even so, the days of the years of my life have been evil. All that I have acquired is vanity; it has not brought me the blessing I longed for. And now that I have lost it all, now that I have given up everything, even Benjamin, this day *YHWH* has truly blessed me![12] My son, I will no longer seek my blessings. I will give up everything that I once considered gain and count it all loss.[13] I no longer need it; I no longer need honor and wealth in order to be truly blessed.

"You see, this day we have left behind our homeland, the land that *YHWH* had promised me to inherit,[14] and we have become strangers in the land of Egypt. But it is well. Before we came down to Egypt, the Elohim of my father spoke to me and taught me to trust. He is faithful to fulfill His promises. Now I understand that it is of no use to run after their fulfillment in my own wisdom and strength. 'I will go down with you to Egypt, and I will also surely bring you up,' He promised me.[15] I wonder what exactly He meant by that.

"Could He mean that He will lead me back to Canaan? Or did He rather mean a better homeland, our real homeland? As long we are on earth, we will always be pilgrims and strangers, even in Canaan.[16] What I now seek and desire is a more excellent heritage, a heavenly homeland that Elohim has prepared for us. It is there where I know He will lead me and bring me up.

"My son, when I look back on my life, I regret and repent for having set my eyes on the same blessings the nations seek.[17] But I will no longer seek after such things. I will set my mind on things above, not on things on earth. *YHWH* has chosen us to be His own people, and I do not want Him to be ashamed to be called *our* Elohim, the Elohim of Abraham, Isaac, and Israel."[18]

Oh, how much his words sounded like the words my grandfather used to speak to me! I felt intense joy at seeing how the road of affliction that he had walked, this valley of the shadow of death that *YHWH* had led him through, had worked in him such an eternal weight of glory.[19]

After this, it was time for my family to meet the king. A few of my brothers went with me to formally request permission to reside in our country. The king welcomed them with open arms and granted them the right to possess land in Goshen, in an area named Rameses. That area was considered the best pastureland that we had. He also told them that if there were good cattlemen among them, he would be happy to pay them to take care of his herds.

Then I wanted the king to meet my father. It was such an extraordinary scene to see this old man talking with

Pharaoh. He shared how his days had been evil, recognizing his failures and errors. Then he stood up and spoke a blessing over the king. My father, blessing the king of Egypt! Is it not always the lesser who is being blessed by the greater?[20] My whole life, I have loved and respected my father, but now I admired him and felt proud to be his son.

When I Saw Their Faces

Chapter 6

The Reform

Management of the Provisions

By the end of the third year of the famine, all private stockrooms in the country were empty, and the land did not yield any crops or fruit anymore. The drought had become so severe that even many fruit trees had started to die. From the beginning of the fourth year on, practically every household in our country totally depended on the provisions from our storehouses. At the end of each year, we took an inventory to see if we needed to adjust our policies concerning the granted ration per person and per household, and also whether we could afford to continue providing for the increasing number of foreigners who came to buy. Our estimations always came out favorably, and we experienced the blessing of Elohim upon us. In the course of the fifth year, however, rumors reached me that many people were concerned about their finances.

During one of our meetings, the officers who managed the local storehouses informed me, "People have come to us and let us know that they will not have enough money to survive if indeed this drought is going to last another two years."

"Should we lower the prices, or will we give the grain away for free once the people are without money?" some counselors wondered.

***

I had thought much about why Elohim had brought this disaster on the world. I meditated on everything that had happened with Father and with my brothers and me, and how Elohim had made all things work together for good: my coming to Egypt many years before the drought; the way Elohim had led me to become the ruler of Egypt; how the famine had caused my brothers to come to me; how they had humbled themselves; and how in the end, all this had led to our reconciliation and to the restoration of my father's house. My brothers and even my father would never be the same. The trials Elohim had led them through—the trials He had led *us* through—had forever changed our hearts.

Considering all these good things that had resulted from the famine made it easy for me to see that Elohim had used it to fulfill His purposes in us. This also helped me to believe that He surely had a plan for my father's household, having brought them out of Canaan to Egypt. I was convinced that He had a purpose for having established them here, even though I could not understand what that purpose was. I knew that there would surely come a day when *YHWH* would call them back to the land that He promised to my fathers as an everlasting inheritance.

Even though I saw that *YHWH* had used the famine to fulfill great purposes in my family, I had a growing feeling that this was not the only reason for this catastrophe. In the following years, as the famine continued, my assumption that Elohim still had other goals to achieve grew into a conviction. One of the most significant lessons that *YHWH* had taught me through all these years was that the Elohim of Abraham, Isaac, and Israel was also the Elohim of Egypt. Therefore, would He not have great purposes for this nation as well? I could not believe that Elohim had brought this famine on the whole world only thinking of us, the children of Abraham.

I think that it was around this time that I started getting the feeling that the heavenly bodies in my second dream could have represented the people of Egypt. Could it be that, now that my first dream had been fulfilled, there was still another purpose lying before me—a calling that I had not fully understood yet, a task that I had not finished yet? Elohim had brought my brothers under my responsibility and care in order to bring restoration to my family. Could it be that He had also put Egypt under my responsibility and care to bring restoration to this nation? And had I not once promised that I would not withhold the rod and the staff of guidance and correction from those whom *YHWH* would put under my responsibility and care, no matter how loudly my emotions protested?

***

"No, we will not lower the prices, and we will not distribute the food for free," I answered.

"Do you want the people to starve, then, while there is plenty of grain in the storehouses?" one of the officers replied.

"No, surely not. Come back tomorrow. I need to talk with *YHWH* first." As always, He was my source of counsel.

"O *YHWH*, You have made me lord over Your household. You have put me over this people, Your people, and established me as a teacher for their elders and as a ruler over their chiefs. You have given me the responsibility to give them food in due season. I have learned to love them and desire to be a blessing to them. Now, teach me and guide me, for I desire to be loyal and faithful to You and fulfill the responsibility You have given me. What must I do to help them further and to lead them on this road of healing and restoration? Speak to me, give me your wisdom, and help me understand Your ways."

My steward was the first one to arrive at the meeting that next morning. I could see his sincere interest and love for the people of Egypt, which caused me to feel so supported by him in my responsibilities, even though it was sometimes hard for him to see my ways of fulfilling them.

"So, do you have a plan?" That was his favorite question.

"Yes, but I am not sure if you are going to like it." That was often my answer.

The Reform

"You can count on my support. I think I know you well enough to trust that you love our nation and that the desire of your heart is to bless the people of Egypt."

When all the other officers and counselors had arrived for our meeting, I shared my plan with them.

"Once the people run out of money, send them to me. When they come to me, I will tell them that they can exchange for food whatever they have, like horses and cattle. I will tell them to return to you. They will bring you their livestock, and you will accept those in trade for food. Before you return to your cities, we will establish the norms by which the trading will take place."

"My lord, what are we going to do with all those animals? They are as lean and ugly as the cows of the king's dream. What good are they to us? What are we going to feed them?"

"They are not of any use to us; they are a burden to us. But this is what we need to do. We are not seeking our own welfare; we are here for the people."

"I have a question, my lord," one of the counselors replied. "Why do we need to collect all the money of the entire country? Where is all that money going?"

"The money goes to the treasury of the king."[1]

"Well, what does the king need all that money for? What does he do for the country? He does not even care about the people. His next meal is the only thing he cares about."

Everybody was silent. "You will never in your life talk about the king this way again!" I replied, looking sharply at him. "Who was it who took the initiative for this entire undertaking? Was it not the king? Could he not just as easily have made sure to collect enough food for himself and his own family, once he knew what was coming? Why was he so concerned when God revealed to him what was coming? Was it not for the well-being of the people of Egypt? The fact that we are here today doing what we are doing—is that not because the king gave us that charge?"

"I apologize, my lord. I had not seen it that way. Honestly, since I never see him at our meetings, it just seemed to me that he does not do anything for the people."

"That is how most people think. But let me explain something to you. See now how this kingdom functions—well, at least how this kingdom must function. In the dreams, God spoke to our king, showing him the responsibilities that He is putting in his hands to care for the people, God's people. And what did the king do? First he went out of every normal way of doing things to come to understand the meaning of the vision. Next, when he realized that he needed support to fulfill these responsibilities, he appointed us to be his helpers. So the king depends on our loyalty in order for him to be able to fulfill his responsibilities before God.

"Now listen. You were there when he set me over the country. Do you remember what he said? '*Only in regard to the throne will I be greater than you,*' he said. Do you know what that means?"

"It means that he still assumes all responsibility," my steward replied before the protester or anybody else could answer.

"Exactly. I use *his* seal to confirm my decisions; I do not have my own seal. The king accepts the responsibility for every decision I make. Can you see how much the king depends on our loyalty and faithfulness?"

I could see in his face that he understood and accepted my correction.

"But still, my lord," another counselor said, "even though I do not want to oppose your decision, I still have a question. Many of us do not understand why the king needs all that money. What is he going to do with it?" Then I shared some more of what God had shown me, although I could not explain everything in detail at this point. Many factors depended on how the people would respond.

"I need you to trust that it will be needed and used for the restoration of the honor and glory of Egypt, and I need everybody's full cooperation to bring this to fulfillment."

The Final Years

At the beginning of the sixth year, representatives of the people from the entire country came to my office. "We have come to inform you that we, the people, have no money anymore. The officers of the storehouses will not give us any food if we cannot pay for it. They told us to come and see you. You must give us grain, because we and our wives and children are hungry. If you do not give us grain, we will die right here in your presence. Is that what you want?"²

"Well, if you do not have any money anymore, what do you have?"

"What do we have? We have cattle and horses, and some people have sheep and donkeys."

"Good. Bring your horses and cattle or whatever you have to the officers who are in charge of the storage in your city. They will trade every animal for a corresponding amount of grain according to its weight." I could sense that there was an attitude of disagreement among them.

"My lord, is it fair that we are being bereaved of our money and assets?" some of them asked.

"Fair?" I responded. "Who then are you blaming for being unfair? God, who brought the famine on our land? Where would you have been if God in His mercy had not given the vision to the king? Or are you blaming the king? Where would you have been if the king had not pursued to understand the vision given to him? Where would you have been if the king had not cared about you, and if he had only cared for himself and his family, leaving you without bread? Acknowledge this day that God has confirmed the king and his kingship over us by showing him how to guide and direct his country through the greatest catastrophe that has ever come on Egypt. The king has accepted the responsibility of delivering his people from perishing, knowing that you would not voluntarily support one another. Acknowledge that you have never had a sense

The Reform

of duty at all for the support of your king and your nation. Be grateful for the great deliverance that this food conservation program has brought to you and your households."

After they all left, my steward came to me. "To anyone else, it would seem that you are still angry with the people of Egypt for the way we treated you when you were a slave and for having thrown you in prison. But I have known you long enough to know that that is not the case. Nevertheless, honestly, I still do not quite understand your plans and where this all is going."

That entire year, the people could buy grain for the value of their livestock. Then came the final year. When they had no animals to trade anymore, my officers sent them to me for the second time. When I saw their faces, I could see that their eyes were full of anguish.

"My lord," they said, "we want you to know that there is no food left in our homes, there is no money left anywhere in Egypt, and all our horses and cattle have become yours. All that is left over are our bodies and our land. Today we come before you with a proposal— a proposal that we and all the people of Egypt have agreed on. We ask you to buy us. Buy our bodies and our land. Buy us for grain, and let us become slaves of Pharaoh. We will serve the king, and we ask you to give us food. This way we and our children will not die, and the land will not become desolate."[3]

I had to run to my inner room and allow myself to weep. What a difference, what a change in their hearts! How could these proud men, who had once thought of themselves as being on the top of the world, humble themselves so deeply as to offer themselves as slaves? It was very hard for me to hear them talk like this. How much did the look in their eyes remind me of that of my brothers the day when they had lost all hope that they would ever go home again! How much their words reminded me of those of Judah, when he had offered himself with a broken and contrite heart to take Benjamin's place and become my slave! Only the hand and Spirit of El Shaddai could have caused such a change.

"Be strong now; you are not finished yet," I told myself when I returned from my chamber. My steward looked at me and noticed the expression on my face.

"Are your emotions protesting?" he whispered.

Then, back in my role as the harsh lord of the land, I replied, "I accept your proposal. I will buy each of you for the king—you, your families, and your land—and I will provide all the grain you need for you and for your households."

They bowed deeply and replied, "You have saved our lives; we will be slaves of the king."

The following days, I had many meetings with all the officers. "This is going to be a major reform in our country. When you go through the land to buy each family, you need to instruct them to abandon their land and move to the cities. There we will give them the instructions for where and how they will be serving the king. In the course of the year, all of Egypt must be moved to the cities."[4] We established fair prices for every person we would buy (according to their age and condition) and for the land.

The Reform

"Buy us for grain," they had said, but we bought them and their land for money, for a fair price. I took the money from the treasury of the king and gave it to the officers so that they could pay for each person and for each field.

"My lord, I do not quite understand your plan," one of the officers said. "Did you not say that the money was going to be used for the restoration of the pride and glory of Egypt? It seems to me that we are rather breaking the pride and glory of our people by making them all slaves and reducing them to servitude."

"No, I did not say that. I said, '*the honor and glory of Egypt.*' Pride and glory do not go together, not for very long at least. If, by the grace of God, our way of using the money will serve to break the *pride* of Egypt, then we have hope and faith that it will also serve to restore the *glory* of Egypt."

During the course of that year, we bought every man in Egypt and all the land, except for the land that was possessed by the priests, since they never had to buy food. By the end of the year, every family was living in the cities. Then I called the representatives of the people from all the cities to my office. When they came to me, I could see the fear in their eyes about what their fate would be. When they all were gathered in my presence, I spoke to them.

"Today, I have bought each of you, your families, and your land for the king. Therefore, it is now the king who will decide, according to his pleasure, what is going to happen with you and with the land." They all agreed and recognized that the king had the right to do so.

"Well, then, this is what the king has decided, and this is what you will do. Go and return to the land that you have sold. Here, take seeds to plant the fields. When you harvest your crops, give one-fifth to the king as tax to contribute to the expenses of his government, for his programs for the advancement of the nation, and for the security and protection of the kingdom. The other four-fifths you may keep for yourselves, to feed your households, to plant your fields, and to build up your estates."[5]

They could not believe their ears!

"Yes, lord, you have saved our lives; we will be servants of the king" is all they could say. They just stood there without knowing what to do; it was not real to them. They had had no hope at all that this would end well for them—no expectation that they would ever receive their freedom back.

"Go now; go back to your land, you and your families. Just remember to be loyal to the king. He is God's servant whom He has set over us for our own good.[6] Respect that; pay the taxes that are required, according to the law that will be valid from this day on. One-fifth of your increase you will give to the king.[7]

"Go now; you are free. Go and tell the people in the cities to return to their homes and to plant their fields as they have always done. The seven years have passed, the famine is over, and our God will bless your fields and provide water for your crops."

Once more, they bowed down and said, "Yes, lord, you have saved our lives; yes, we will surely be faithful servants of the king." Then they left.

The Reform

Seeing the joy in their faces gave me the deepest thankfulness in my heart that you can imagine—thankfulness to Elohim for the enormous privilege He had given me to be a blessing to this nation.

I knew that Egypt was not the same as it had been fourteen years before, and that Egypt would not have been the same if the famine had never happened. Although the food distribution program was over, the reform of the organizational structure and the taxation laws were permanent. The officers whom I had established in each city remained in office; they were in charge of collecting the tax in their corresponding provinces. So, in essence, the reform that was initially a response to the famine had caused a permanent solidification of the kingdom, which gave the king the power and the means that he needed to adequately fulfill his responsibilities before God.

The most important result of the famine, however, was not the reform of the system but the transformation in the hearts of the people. The hardships and trials they had gone through had caused a change in their attitudes toward the king and toward one another. They recognized the authority of the king and accepted their own responsibility for the functioning of the kingdom. Furthermore, the many teachings and discussions that I had had with the elders, officers, and counselors had brought a new understanding of what a kingdom actually is and how it operates. This understanding had caused a change in the way they served the king and the kingdom. They had learned to acknowledge that God is sovereign over all kingdoms on earth and that He establishes kings over them as He desires.[8]

"So does that mean that the king is always right?" my steward asked me once. "When a kingdom turns into anarchy or tyranny, is that always the fault of the people, their lack of loyalty and faithfulness? Can it not be the fault of the king, even if God has put him there?"

I remember that we sat down and talked for a long time about this question. "Here in Egypt, we are blessed, because our king is a man who fears God," I said. "You have seen that, in times when he feels that he lacks the wisdom and experience to rule or the discernment to judge, he appoints people he believes he can trust to support him in this task. The reason he does that is because he recognizes that he has the responsibility before God to rule and to judge.

"However, if God ever raised up a king in Egypt who would deny Him and say, 'Who is God? I do not know any God,' then Egypt would surely turn into a tyranny."[9]

My steward asked, "So why would God raise up such a king?[10] Do you think that is fair? Should we not be allowed to reject such a king and be able to choose the king we want?"

"Fair? You did not get to choose your own father and mother; is that unfair? Why does God give God-fearing parents to some and tyrannical parents to others? Why does He raise up God-fearing kings at certain times and places, and tyrannical kings at others? We must believe that He will give us the king whom we need or deserve and that whatever He does, He does so for His purposes and for our good. At the moment, we may not always understand His motives—why He brings certain circumstances to us, or allows certain things to happen to us. But we do not need to. What we *do* need to understand is how to *respond* to those circumstances. And He is surely faithful to teach us that, if we truly desire to walk in His ways. Have we not experienced that during these last fourteen years?"

These and many more memories went through my mind as I saw the representatives leaving my office, returning to the cities where the people were waiting to hear the instructions. In my mind's eye, I could see all their faces at the moment when they would hear the news, when the representatives would tell them, "We are free! We are going home!"

When I Saw Their Faces

Chapter 7

Final Words

Many years have passed since the days of the famine. To this day, I have continued serving the king, but more as a counselor than as a ruler. After all the people had returned to their possessions, I gave the final report to the king. There were still funds in the treasury after we had bought all the land and all the people, also because much foreign money had come in.

"All the people and all the land are yours now, my king," I said.

"Rather, they are God's," he replied, "but He has set me over His household, and I accept that responsibility as His faithful servant."[1]

Then he asked me about my father and brothers. "What are they going to do? Do they want to return to Canaan? Tell them that they are welcome to stay in Goshen. They are a blessing to me and to Egypt."

"*They are a blessing,*" he had said. Is this not what it is all about? We, the chosen people—we did not come to Egypt to be blessed; we came to be a blessing![2]

"I will go and ask them."

***

"No, we will remain here until *YHWH* calls us," my father answered when I asked him about his plans. "When my grandfather left the land of the Chaldeans and started his journey to Canaan, he did so because El Shaddai called him. When I left Padan Aram to return to Canaan, I did so because *YHWH* called me in a dream. When I left Canaan to come to Egypt, I came because *YHWH* spoke to me in Beersheba.[3] Now, I will not leave Egypt and return to Canaan unless and until *YHWH* speaks to me. I know that Canaan is the land that He has promised me as an eternal inheritance, but I am not worried about that. He will surely fulfill this promise in His time, and we will be ready to obey whenever He calls."

Father still lived another twelve years after the famine ended. He became a very well-respected man in Egypt, just as his father and grandfather had been in Canaan. When he died, all of Egypt mourned for seventy days, which is in accordance with the number of days the people of Egypt mourn for their kings. Then we took his body to Canaan.

"Promise me that, when *YHWH* takes my soul up to my heavenly homeland, you will take my body to my earthly homeland," he had said to all of us. "Bury me in the cave of Machpelah, where the bones of my fathers are buried, and also the bones of Leah." Pharaoh sent all his important people with me to Canaan.

His burial was a day of very great and heavy lamentation, as only the greatest men are honored with. "*I do not need honor and wealth anymore in order to be blessed,"* he had told me. However, never in his life had he been a man of such honor as during the years when he lived here in Egypt!

And now, I have become an old man myself, "and I do not know the day of my death," as my grandfather used to say. I know some find it strange that, even though there was a time when I had all the money of Egypt in my power, and even though I bought all the land of Egypt, today I do not have a place for my bones to be buried. Well, actually, I do have a place, but not in Egypt, I mean. Did I tell you that my father had bought a field from the people of Shechem? That is the area where we first settled when we came from Padan Aram to Canaan, the field that we had to abandon shortly after he bought it. It really is a nice piece of land, near the place where my brothers were herding the sheep when they sold me. It even has a well—no, not the dry well where they threw me in; it has a good well with clear water. Well, I inherited that field.[4]

You probably remember what I told you in the beginning about my father, how he always wanted me to be the heir to his possessions. He also always thought of me as the future chief of his descendants. That never happened. Obviously, I was in a position of authority over them during my years as lord of the land, but what I mean is that I never ended up inheriting my father's place as the patriarch and ruler of our tribe.

Sometimes I wonder whom *YHWH* has chosen to become the real heir. I am not sure, but the last words that my father spoke over all of us made me think. When it was my brother Judah's turn, I heard my father prophesying that the lordship would never depart from him and from his descendants and that all his brothers would come to praise him. That made me wonder if Judah could be the one through whom the Blessing of Abraham finally and in all its perfection will be fulfilled.[5]

But what was I going to say about my burial? Oh yes…I gave instructions to my children to take my bones to that piece of land that I inherited from my father. "Elohim will surely visit you and take you to the land He promised to our fathers," I told them. "When that day comes, take my bones with you and bury me there."[6]

I do not have an inheritance in Egypt. *"You will die as poor as you came,"* the slaves at Potiphar's house had told me once. They were right. I have no earthly possessions here to leave to my children. The legacy that I hope to leave with them is that they will not desire earthly possessions, but that they may desire the heavenly inheritance that Elohim Himself has prepared for them. There is no greater thing that I can leave as an inheritance to them than that they will know *YHWH* and understand His ways…that they will not fear when He leads them through valleys of the shadow of death, knowing that He is always with them to guide them according to His perfect will—according to His design and purposes.

Once, when he was still little, one of my boys asked me, "Father, where did you learn to become a ruler? Did you go to a school for that?"

Final Words

I thought for a moment, and then I said, "Yes. That is right; I went to a school for that. Elohim sent me to a school for that—to various schools, actually. One school was in Canaan, where I learned to be loyal and faithful to my father, who was my king at that time. I learned to be faithful, even when my loyalty could cause great harm to myself.

"Another school was the time when I worked for Mr. Potiphar, my next king. There I learned to serve, heartily, as for Elohim and not for men, without any expectation of rewards or benefits. All the fruit of my work was for my master; he was the one who received all the honor and profit for what I accomplished.[7] If I had not learned that, what do you think I would be doing now with all the money that the people are paying me for the grain? Do you think that I would be putting it all in the treasury of the king? Or would I rather be thinking about how to gain profit for myself?

"And another school was when I was in prison. There I learned to fulfill the orders of my master with all my heart, even when my master had hurt me—when he had treated me with unrighteousness.

"There, I also learned to look into the eyes and see the faces of those who were under my care. I learned to see their needs and their trouble, even though I had much trouble myself. And I learned to care about their dreams, even though I had my own dreams that were not being fulfilled.

"That is what a ruler has to learn, my son. Above everything else, a ruler must be faithful and loyal to his king, and in the second place, he must be concerned about the needs of those under his rule."

"And what if you are the very king yourself?"

"Then *YHWH* is your king. Every king must be faithful and loyal to Him. He is the Creator of all; all the kingdoms of the world are His. He is the King of all kings and the Lord of all lords."

That night, I thought much about the questions my son had asked and about the answers that I had given him. I suddenly realized that everything I had considered adversities at the time—obstacles that were against me, preventing me from reaching my goals and dreams—all those things, in fact, had been the very schools that *YHWH* had chosen for me, to prepare me for the mission that He had called me to!

In each of these schools, I had been surrounded by people who did not care about my dreams, desires, needs, or even suffering. At times, I allowed my self-pity to control my life, until I learned that my real bondage and prison were my own dreams and goals. I learned that my freedom did not depend on my circumstances. In fact, during my time in prison, I was set free long before the gates were opened.

Once the chains of my selfishness were broken, I was free to see the faces of those around me. Then I saw that I was surrounded by many others who were also in slavery or in prison and who also had their own dreams!

Now, looking back on my life, I can see how vital and decisive it was to reach that freedom. Just think of it:

Final Words

What if I had not looked at the cupbearer and the baker—what if I had not seen their faces? I would not have noticed the trouble in their eyes, and I would not have asked them what was going on. They would never have shared their dreams, so I would never have shared the interpretation. The cupbearer would have returned to the king anyway, and the baker would have been executed just as well. The fact that they told me their dreams and that I gave the interpretations did not make any difference. However, the cupbearer would not have mentioned me on the day when the king had his dream, and I would have spent the rest of my life in prison.

Do you see how Elohim let my whole future depend on that one question, whether or not I would see the faces of the cupbearer and the baker and notice the sadness in their eyes?

"Could He not have brought you out of prison another way then?" you might ask.

Yes, He surely could have. But why would He? If I had remained bound by the chains of my selfishness and therefore not been free to watch and see the faces of those around me, of those whom *YHWH* put under my care, I would not have been of any use to Him in the mission He had for me: the mission to be used by Him to be a true blessing to those whom He would bring onto my path.

Now I can see that the faithfulness and presence of *YHWH* have never failed. He surely is the One who lives and sees me, He never slumbers nor sleeps. Now I see how, from the day when I became a slave, He has led me on this journey to true freedom, a road of emptying myself from being the beloved—the heir, the preferred—to making myself nothing.[8] I can see how He has led me by teaching me to become a loyal servant of the Egyptians, whom I, deep in my heart, had despised as not being part of the chosen of *YHWH*. And then, He took me even one step further, leading me to become a humble servant of the very lowest among the Egyptians—the criminals, the outcast.

Not until I had reached that true freedom could I become useful in His hands to lead others on this same journey. It was then when He brought my brothers back in my life, and used me to bring these once-so-arrogant men to the point where they humbled themselves and offered themselves to become slaves. And next, He brought all those proud Egyptians to me and used me to lead them on this same road. At the end, they also humbled themselves—they too came to the point where they offered themselves to become slaves!

I surely hope that I am not giving the impression that I am bragging about being such a wonderful person. I trust you can see that what I want to emphasize is the *wisdom* of *YHWH* to teach us and to correct us, in order to equip us for the good works He has prepared for us, and the *power* of El Shaddai to use even the worst circumstances and cause them to work together for good, according to His eternal purposes. With His wisdom and power, He transforms us into the people He wants us to be, like a potter molds and shapes the clay to transform it into a good and beautiful vessel.[9]

This story is not about me; it is about *YHWH*. As you have seen, He did not transform only me. He also transformed my brothers, my father, and even the king and the nation of Egypt. Therefore, I hope that my story may be an encouragement to you. Sooner or later you may identify with me in any of the conditions I have gone through.

Someday, you too may be surrounded by brothers and even a father who do not believe in your dreams. Or you may be serving a Potiphar who is, as you see it, only interested in his own next meal. Maybe you will feel imprisoned, by people or by conditions, and be without any hope that your circumstances will ever become favorable for you. At times, you may even feel forsaken by Elohim! And just as I was, at times you may be confused by those situations, especially when they are so contrary to the things you had hoped for and believed in, maybe even based on the dreams and promises from Elohim. If, in those times, remembering my trials helps you know how to respond to yours, and see that *YHWH* your Elohim surely is El Shaddai—the Almighty One who lives and sees you—it will not have been in vain that I told you my story.

Joseph

Notes and References

Chapter 1: Notes and References

1. Hebrews 11:14.

    For those who say such things declare plainly that they seek a homeland.

2. Genesis 30:25–30.

    *Jacob said to Laban, "Send me away, that I may go to my own place and to my country...You know how I have served you and how your livestock has been with me. For what you had before I came was little, and it has increased to a great amount; the L*ORD *has blessed you since my coming. And now, when shall I also provide for my own house?"*

3. Genesis 49:3–7.

    Reuben...you shall not excel, Because you went up to your father's bed; Then you defiled it — He went up to my couch. Simeon and Levi are brothers; Instruments of cruelty are in their dwelling place. Let not my soul enter their council; Let not my honor be united to their assembly; For in their anger they slew a man, And in their self-will they hamstrung an ox. Cursed be their anger, for it is fierce; And their wrath, for it is cruel! I will divide them in Jacob and scatter them in Israel.

Notes and References

4. Genesis 37:2.

    This is the history of Jacob. Joseph, being seventeen years old, was feeding the flock with his brothers. And the lad was with the sons of Bilhah and the sons of Zilpah, his father's wives; and Joseph brought a bad report of them to his father.

5. Genesis 37:3

    Although many Bible versions translate, *"a coat of many colors,"* apparently following the (Greek) Septuagint text, the original Hebrew text seems to indicate that it rather was a coat that reached to his feet.

6. Compare Genesis 37:25, 36, and 39:1.

    The merchants who bought Joseph were descendants of Ishmael and Midian, who were sons of Abraham, half brothers of Isaac.

7. Genesis 44:27.

    Then your servant my father said to us, "You know that my wife bore me two sons;"

8. Compare Psalm 139:23–24.

    Search me, O God, and know my heart: try me, and know my thoughts: And see if there be any wicked way in me... (KJV)

    Even though in the previous verses he expresses his own righteous attitude, David acknowledges that only God knows the real and deepest motives of our hearts.

9. Genesis 34:25.

    Now it came to pass on the third day, when they were in pain, that two of the sons of Jacob, Simeon and Levi, Dinah's brothers, each took his sword and came boldly upon the city and killed all the males.

Chapter 2: Notes and References

1. Genesis 24:7.

    "The LORD God of heaven..."

    The literal Hebrew text has "*heavens*" as plural.

2. Genesis 28:13.

    And behold, the LORD stood above it and said: "I am the LORD God of Abraham your father and the God of Isaac; the land on which you lie I will give to you and your descendants..."

3. Genesis 26:24.

    And the LORD appeared to him the same night and said, "I am the God of your father Abraham..."

4. Genesis 31:30.

    And now you have surely gone because you greatly long for your father's house, but why did you steal my gods?

5. Genesis 31:19.

    Now Laban had gone to shear his sheep, and Rachel had stolen the household idols [Hebrew: Teraphim] *that were her father's.*

6. Genesis 35:2.

    And Jacob said to his household and to all who were with him, "Put away the foreign gods that are among you, purify yourselves, and change your garments."

7. Genesis 28:4.

    And give you the blessing of Abraham...

    Galatians 3:14.

    that the blessing of Abraham might come upon the Gentiles in Christ Jesus...

Notes and References

8. Genesis 17:14.

    And the uncircumcised male child, who is not circumcised in the flesh of his foreskin, that person shall be cut off from his people; he has broken My covenant.

9. Genesis 26:4. God speaks to Isaac:

    And I will make your descendants multiply as the stars of heaven; I will give to your descendants all these lands; and in your seed all the nations of the earth shall be blessed;

10. Psalm 105:9–10.

    The covenant which He made with Abraham, And His oath to Isaac, And confirmed it to Jacob for a statute, To Israel as an everlasting covenant,

11. Genesis 16:13–14.

    Then she called the name of the LORD who spoke to her, You-Are-the-God-Who-Sees; for she said, "Have I also here seen Him who sees me?" Therefore the well was called Beer Lahai Roi...

    Lahai Roi means: "the One who lives and sees me."

12. Psalm 32:8–9.

    I will instruct you and teach you in the way you should go; I will guide you with My eye. Do not be like the horse or like the mule, Which have no understanding, Which must be harnessed with bit and bridle, Else they will not come near you.

    God has the ability to teach us softly and by using force. In this psalm, He expresses His desire for us to not be obstinate, so that He may teach and lead us without needing to use force.

13. Genesis 12:2–3.

    I will make you a great nation; I will bless you and make your name great; And you shall be a blessing. I will bless those who bless you, And I will curse him who curses you; And in you all the families of the earth shall be blessed.

14. Romans 2:11.

    For there is no partiality with God.

15. Romans 3:29.

    Or is He the God of the Jews only? Is He not also the God of the Gentiles? Yes, of the Gentiles also.

16. Genesis 26:28

    But they said, "We have certainly seen that the L<small>ORD</small> is with you. So we said, "Let there now be an oath between us, between you and us; and let us make a covenant with you..."

17. Romans 2:24.

    For "the name of God is blasphemed among the Gentiles because of you," as it is written.

    Through our actions, God's people either cause His name to be glorified or cause it to be blasphemed among those who do not know Him.

    Compare also Ezekiel 36:20–23; 1Timothy 6:1; Titus 2:5; Matthew 5:16.

18. Compare Matthew 6:32–33.

    For after all these things the Gentiles seek...But seek first the kingdom of God.

19. Hebrews 11:8.

    By faith Abraham obeyed when he was called to go out to the place which he would receive as an inheritance. And he went out, not knowing where he was going.

20. Genesis 26:12–13

    Then Isaac sowed in that land, and reaped in the same year a hundredfold; and the L<small>ORD</small> blessed him. The man began *to prosper, and continued prospering until he became very prosperous; for he had possessions of flocks and possessions of herds and a great number of servants.*

21. Compare James 1:2.

    ...count it all joy when you fall into various trials.

22. Compare Philippians 4:7.

    and the peace of God, which surpasses all understanding, will guard your hearts and minds through Christ Jesus.

23. Compare 2 Corinthians 10:4–5.

    For the weapons of our warfare are not carnal but mighty in God for pulling down strongholds, casting down arguments and every high thing that exalts itself against the knowledge of God, bringing every thought into captivity to the obedience of Christ.

24. Genesis 39:4.

    "and served him."

    The Hebrew word here for "*served*" is commonly used for priests ministering to God, or high officers serving a king. It is not usually used for slaves serving their master.

25. Genesis 46:34.

    that you shall say, "Your servants' occupation has been with livestock from our youth even till now, both we and also our fathers,' that you may dwell in the land of Goshen; for every shepherd is an abomination to the Egyptians."

26. Compare 1 Thessalonians 1:9.

    Paul calls God "*the living and true God*" to express the contrast with the false gods of the Gentiles.

27. Genesis 39:3.

    And his master saw that the LORD was with him and that the LORD made all he did to prosper in his hand.

Notes and References

28. Matthew 8:9.

    For I also am a man under authority, having soldiers under me...

    The centurion asserts that his authority over others is based on the fact that he himself is under authority.

29. John 19:11.

    Jesus answered, "You could have no power at all against Me unless it had been given you from above..."

    Jesus asserts that authority can only be given "from above." It is not clear if He means "from God" or "from a higher human authority," which in this case would mean "from Caesar." The reason why Jesus was not specific about this may be to say that both meanings are true.

30. Numbers 16:13.

    Is it a small thing that you have brought us up out of a land flowing with milk and honey, to kill us in the wilderness, that you should keep acting like a prince over us?

    Numbers 12:3.

    (Now the man Moses was very humble, more than all men who were on the face of the earth.)

    Even though the Bible testifies of Moses that he was humbler than any other man on earth, in the eyes of Korah, Dathan, Abiram, and On, he was a man seeking power and elevating himself over the people of Israel.

31. Genesis 37:19.

    Then they said to one another, "Look, this dreamer is coming!"

32. Genesis 39:5.

    So it was, from the time that he had made him overseer of his house and all that he had, that the LORD blessed the Egyptian's house for Joseph's sake; and the blessing of the LORD was on all that he had in the house and in the field.

Chapter 3: Notes and References

1. Colossians 3:17, 23.

   In the beginning, man and wife were joined by God for the purpose of serving Him together, and He established that man is in need of the support from his wife. From the fact that *"whatever we do in word or deed,"* we should do *"in the name of the Lord"* and *"to the Lord"*, it follows that it is God's design that man and wife work together and support each other in everything they do.

2. Psalm 105:18

   They hurt his feet with fetters...

3. Genesis 40:3.

   ...in the house of the captain of the guard, in the prison, the place where Joseph was confined.

4. Genesis 40:15.

   ...I have done nothing here that they should put me into the dungeon.

5. Genesis 39:20.

   Then Joseph's master took him and put him into the prison, a place where the king's prisoners were confined. And he was there in the prison.

6. Genesis 39:6.

   Thus he left all that he had in Joseph's hand, and he did not know what he had except for the bread which he ate...

7. Psalm 109:2.

   A psalm of David in which he struggles with injustice committed against him and learns to trust in God in the midst of these circumstances.

8. Job 38:2.

   Just as He did with Joseph, God allowed very severe conditions in the life of Job. Through these trials, He taught him to not focus on his own pain but to set his eyes on God's sovereignty and his mind on His purposes.

9. Jonah 4:4.

   Just as Joseph did, Jonah had to learn that God loves the Gentile nations just as much as He loves the chosen nation, even when he considers those nations a threat or an enemy.

10. Psalm 139:23.

    Search me, O God, and know my heart: try me, and know my thoughts: (KJV)

11. Genesis 16:9.

    The Angel of the LORD said to her, 'Return to your mistress, and submit yourself under her hand.'

    Hagar, an Egyptian slave, was instructed by the angel to return and to submit to her Hebrew mistress, who had dealt harshly with her. Similarly, Joseph, a Hebrew slave, had to learn to submit to an Egyptian master who had dealt harshly with him.

12. Compare Matthew 5:46.

    For if you love those who love you, what reward have you? Do not even the tax collectors do the same?

13. Compare Isaiah 55:7-9.

    Let the wicked forsake his way, And the unrighteous man his thoughts; Let him return to the LORD...For My thoughts are not your thoughts, Nor are your ways My ways," says the LORD. For as the heavens are higher than the earth, So are My ways higher than your ways, And My thoughts than your thoughts.

Notes and References

14. Compare Job 42:1–6.

    Job shows that he accepts God's teaching by repeating almost the exact words that God had used earlier to correct him.

15. Genesis 22:12.

    And He said, "Do not lay your hand on the lad, or do anything to him; for now I know that you fear God, since you have not withheld your son, your only son, from Me."

16. Genesis 40:4.

    And the captain of the guard charged Joseph with them...

    The order was given by Potiphar personally.

17. Compare 2 Corinthians 10:4–6.

    For the weapons of our warfare are not carnal but mighty in God for pulling down strongholds, casting down arguments and every high thing that exalts itself against the knowledge of God, bringing every thought into captivity to the obedience of Christ, and being ready to punish all disobedience when your obedience is fulfilled.

18. Genesis 40:4.

    "and he served them"

    The Hebrew word here for "*served*" is commonly used for priests ministering to God, or high officers serving a king. It is not usually used for the act of serving as a slave.

19. Genesis 40:6–7.

    And Joseph came in to them in the morning and looked at them, and saw that they were sad. So he asked Pharaoh's officers who were with him in the custody of his lord's house, saying, "Why do you look so sad today?"

    Joseph not only saw the expression of their faces, but he also noticed that they looked different "*today*" than they had the day(s) before.

20. Compare Psalm 51:10–14.

   Create in me a clean heart, O God, And renew a steadfast spirit within me...Deliver me from the guilt of bloodshed, O God, The God of my salvation...

21. Compare Daniel 4:27.

   Therefore, O king, let my advice be acceptable to you; break off your sins by being righteous, and your iniquities by showing mercy...

   These are the words that Daniel used to lead King Nebuchadnezzar to repentance.

22. Compare Genesis 48:18

   When speaking to his father, Joseph calls him "*Abi*" ("*my father*" in Hebrew).

Chapter 4: Notes and References

1. Daniel 2:27–28.

   Daniel answered in the presence of the king, and said, 'The secret which the king has demanded, the wise men, the astrologers, the magicians, and the soothsayers cannot declare to the king. 'But there is a God in heaven who reveals secrets...'

   The similarities between the story of Daniel and that of Joseph are striking. They both learned to love and bless the kings and nations to which they were taken. Comparing their lives and especially the way they responded to their circumstances helps us to discern what the Bible teaches us through these stories.

   Genesis 41:16

   And Joseph answered Pharaoh, saying, It is not in me: God shall give Pharaoh an answer of peace.

2. Compare Daniel 2:20–23.

   Joseph must have felt the same excitement that we can discern in Daniel's words when he experienced that God revealed to him the secrets of the king's dreams.

3. Compare Acts 7:22.

   And Moses was learned in all the wisdom of the Egyptians, and was mighty in words and deeds.

   Even in the time of the patriarchs, Egypt was a highly-developed nation in many areas of science and philosophy, such as mathematics, architecture, agriculture, metallurgy, astronomy, government, arts, etc.

4. James 3:17–18.

   But the wisdom that is from above is first pure, then peaceable, gentle, willing to yield, full of mercy and good fruits, without partiality and without hypocrisy. Now the fruit of righteousness is sown in peace by those who make peace.

Wisdom from above is not (merely) intellectual wisdom; it is what builds our character in the first place. The king saw that the Spirit of God was with Joseph, which caused him to be not only wise and discerning but also—and most importantly—righteous, loyal, and trustworthy.

5. Compare 2 Samuel 3:39.

   And I am weak today, though anointed king; and these men, the sons of Zeruiah, are too harsh for me...

   These are the words of David concerning his great men Joab and Abishai.

   In many stories, the Bible addresses the problem of kings and leaders being too weak to govern those who were actually established to help, serve or counsel them, at times even to the point of yielding to them.

6. Genesis 41:43.

   And he had him ride in the second chariot which he had; and they cried out before him, "Bow the knee!" So he set him over all the land of Egypt.

7. Psalm 105:21–22.

   He made him lord of his house, And ruler of all his possessions, To bind his princes at his pleasure, And teach his elders wisdom."

8. Genesis 45:8.

   "[God] *has made me a father to Pharaoh*"

***

It is certainly surprising that Joseph's first impression of the king was not only that he would not know what to do, but also that he lacked the capacity to deal with the future situation—he needed to appoint someone else, a *"discerning and wise man,"* who would be able to solve the coming problems. This impression—coupled with the fact that Joseph, being a young man himself, felt like a *father to Pharaoh*—is hard to explain by anything other than assuming that Pharaoh must have been very young, or at least inexperienced.

Furthermore, in Psalm 105 we read that Pharaoh made Joseph a ruler to *"bind his princes"* and to *"teach his elders."* The word translated "bind," when used in relation to humans, typically means "put in prison." Considering the fact that two years earlier Pharaoh already had been confronted with rebellious high officers, this makes it very likely that he was facing power struggles with his great men.

***

9. Genesis 41:55.

   Then Pharaoh said to all the Egyptians, "Go to Joseph; whatever he says to you, do."

10. Genesis 41:51–52.

    Joseph called the name of the firstborn Manasseh: "For God has made me forget all my toil and all my father's house." And the name of the second he called Ephraim: "For God has caused me to be fruitful in the land of my affliction."

11. Compare Deuteronomy 11:10–12.

    For the land which you go to possess is not like the land of Egypt from which you have come, where you sowed your seed and watered it by foot, as a vegetable garden; but the land which you cross over to possess is a land of hills and valleys, which drinks water from the rain of heaven, a land for which the LORD *your God cares; the eyes of the* LORD *your God are always on it, from the beginning of the year to the very end of the year.*

These are the words of Moses when he prepares the people of Israel for entering the land of Canaan.

Notes and References

Chapter 5: Notes and References

1. Genesis 42:6–9.

   ...And Joseph's brothers came and bowed down before him with their faces to the earth...Then Joseph remembered the dreams which he had dreamed about them...

2. Psalm 23:3–4.

   He restores my soul; He leads me in the paths of righteousness for His name's sake. Yea, though I walk through the valley of the shadow of death, I will fear no evil; For You are with me; Your rod and Your staff, they comfort me.

3. Daniel 2:46.

   Then King Nebuchadnezzar fell on his face, prostrate before Daniel

   Of all the similarities between the stories of Joseph and Daniel, one of the most significant is that their Gentile kings attributed the virtues that they saw in their Hebrew servants to their God. This brought Nebuchadnezzar to the point of actually kneeling down to Daniel and making him ruler over the whole province of Babylon and chief governor over all his wise men. Although we do not see Pharaoh literally bow down to Joseph, his attitude in this context is surely very similar to that of Nebuchadnezzar.

4. Compare Matthew 24:45.

   Who then is a faithful and wise servant, whom his master made ruler over his household, to give them food in due season?

NOTES AND REFERENCES

5. Genesis 45:8.

    So now it was not you who sent me here, but God; and He has made me a father to Pharaoh, and lord of all his house, and a ruler throughout all the land of Egypt.

6. Genesis 38:7–10.

    But Er, Judah's firstborn, was wicked in the sight of the LORD, and the LORD killed him...And the thing which he [Onan, Judah's second son] did displeased the LORD; therefore He killed him also.

7. Genesis 38:25–26.

    When she was brought out, she sent to her father-in-law, saying, "By the man to whom these belong, I am with child."...So Judah acknowledged them and said, "She has been more righteous than I..."

8. Compare Job 1:22.

    In all this Job did not sin nor charge God with wrong.

9. Isaiah 48:10–13.

    Behold, I have refined you, but not as silver; I have tested you in the furnace of affliction. For My own sake, for My own sake, I will do it...And I will not give My glory to another. "Listen to Me, O Jacob, And Israel, My called: I am He, I am the First, I am also the Last. Indeed My hand has laid the foundation of the earth...

10. Romans 8:28.

    And we know that all things work together for good to those who love God, to those who are the called according to His purpose.

11. Genesis 18:19.

    Abraham taught "*his children and his household after him, that they keep the way of the LORD, to do righteousness and justice.*" His household includes the Gentile slaves whom he had bought or who were born in his house (Genesis 17:27). The story in Genesis 24 is an excellent illustration of how his teachings had shaped the life of the old servant who was sent to find a wife for Isaac. All through the Scriptures, we see that Abraham and his descendants are called and sent to teach the nations the way of the LORD, to do righteousness and justice.

12. Genesis 43:13.

    Take your brother also and go back to the man at once.

    Jacob had to give up Benjamin; he was not stolen from him, like Joseph, or taken away by circumstances beyond his control, like his other possessions.

13. Compare Philippians 3:7–8.

    But what things were gain to me, these I have counted loss for Christ. Yet indeed I also count all things loss for the excellence of the knowledge of Christ Jesus my Lord, for whom I have suffered the loss of all things, and count them as rubbish, that I may gain Christ

14. Genesis 28:13.

    the land on which you lie I will give to you and your descendants.

15. Genesis 46:4.

    "I will go down with you to Egypt, and I will also surely bring you up again; and Joseph will put his hand on your eyes."

16. Hebrews 11:13

    These all died in faith, not having received the promises, but having seen them afar off were assured of them, embraced them and confessed that they were strangers and pilgrims on the earth.

Notes and References

17. Compare Matthew 6:31-33.

    Therefore do not worry, saying, 'What shall we eat?' or 'What shall we drink?' or 'What shall we wear?' For after all these things the Gentiles seek. But seek first the kingdom of God and His righteousness.

18. Hebrews 11:16.

    But now they desire a better, that is, a heavenly country. Therefore God is not ashamed to be called their God...

19. Compare 2 Corinthians 4:17.

    For our light affliction, which is but for a moment, is working for us a far more exceeding and eternal weight of glory.

20. Compare Hebrews 7:7.

    Now beyond all contradiction the lesser is blessed by the better.

Chapter 6: Notes and References

1. Genesis 47:14.

   And Joseph gathered up all the money that was found in the land of Egypt and in the land of Canaan, for the grain which they bought; and Joseph brought the money into Pharaoh's house.

2. Genesis 47:15.

   So when the money failed in the land of Egypt and in the land of Canaan, all the Egyptians came to Joseph and said, "Give us bread, for why should we die in your presence? For the money has failed."

3. Genesis 47:18–19.

   When that year had ended, they came to him the next year and said to him, "We will not hide from my lord that our money is gone; my lord also has our herds of livestock. There is nothing left in the sight of my lord but our bodies and our lands. Why should we die before your eyes, both we and our land? Buy us and our land for bread, and we and our land will be servants of Pharaoh; give us seed, that we may live and not die, that the land may not be desolate."

4. Genesis 47:21.

   And as for the people, he moved them into the cities, from one end of the borders of Egypt to the other end.

5. Genesis 47:23–24.

   Then Joseph said to the people, "Indeed I have bought you and your land this day for Pharaoh. Look, here is seed for you, and you shall sow the land. And it shall come to pass in the harvest that you shall give one-fifth to Pharaoh. Four-fifths shall be your own, as seed for the field and for your food, for those of your households and as food for your little ones."

6. Compare Romans 13:4, 7.

   For he is God's minister to you for good…

   Render therefore to all their due: taxes to whom taxes are due, customs to whom customs, fear to whom fear, honor to whom honor.

7. Genesis 47:26.

   And Joseph made it a law over the land of Egypt to this day, that Pharaoh should have one-fifth, except for the land of the priests only, which did not become Pharaoh's.

8. Compare Daniel 4:25.

   …seven times shall pass over you, till you know that the Most High rules in the kingdom of men, and gives it to whomever He chooses.

   The literal text says, "*…whomever He desires.*"

9. Compare Exodus 5:2.

   And Pharaoh said, "Who is the LORD, that I should obey His voice to let Israel go? I do not know the LORD, nor will I let Israel go."

10. Romans 9:17.

    For the Scripture says to Pharaoh, "For this very purpose I have raised you up, that I may show My power in you, and that My name may be declared in all the earth."

    See also Exodus 9:16

Chapter 7: Notes and References

1. Compare Matthew 24:45.

   Who then is a faithful and wise servant, whom his master made ruler over his household, to give them food in due season?

2. Genesis 47:7, 10.

   Then Joseph brought in his father Jacob and set him before Pharaoh; and Jacob blessed Pharaoh...So Jacob blessed Pharaoh, and went out from before Pharaoh.

3. Genesis 46:1–6.

   So Israel took his journey with all that he had, and came to Beersheba, and offered sacrifices to the God of his father Isaac...So He said, "I am God, the God of your father; do not fear to go down to Egypt...I will go down with you to Egypt...Then Jacob arose from Beersheba...and went to Egypt, Jacob and all his descendants with him.

4. John 4:5–6.

   So He [Jesus] came to a city of Samaria which is called Sychar, near the plot of ground that Jacob gave to his son Joseph. Now Jacob's well was there...

   Sychar is the New Testament name of Shechem.

5. Genesis 49:8–10.

   Judah, you are he whom your brothers shall praise...The scepter shall not depart from Judah, Nor a lawgiver from between his feet, Until Shiloh comes; And to Him shall be the obedience of the people.

   Acts 3:25–26.

   You are sons of the prophets, and of the covenant which God made with our fathers, saying to Abraham, "And in your seed all the families of the earth shall be blessed." To you first, God, having raised up His Servant Jesus, sent Him to bless you...

Galatians 3:16

Now to Abraham and his Seed were the promises made. He does not say, "And to seeds," as of many, but as of one, "And to your Seed," who is Christ.

The Blessing of Abraham is fulfilled through Jesus, who, as to His earthly life, was a descendant of Judah. However, in Genesis 28:14, God says to Jacob that all the families of the earth shall be blessed "*in you and in your seed.*" From this we understand that God also intends that His chosen people should themselves be a blessing as well.

6. Genesis 50:25.

   Then Joseph took an oath from the children of Israel, saying, "God will surely visit you, and you shall carry up my bones from here."

   See also Joshua 24:32.

7. Compare Colossians 3:22–24.

   Bondservants, obey in all things your masters according to the flesh, not with eyeservice, as men-pleasers, but in sincerity of heart, fearing God. And whatever you do, do it heartily, as to the Lord and not to men, knowing that from the Lord you will receive the reward of the inheritance; for you serve the Lord Christ.

8. Compare Philippians 2:5–7.

   Let this mind be in you which was also in Christ Jesus...who...but made Himself of no reputation, [Literal: *who emptied Himself*] *taking the form of a bondservant, and coming in the likeness of men.*

9. Compare Jeremiah 18:4.

    And the vessel that he made of clay was marred in the hand of the potter; so he made it again into another vessel, as it seemed good to the potter to make.

www.ingramcontent.com/pod-product-compliance
Lightning Source LLC
Chambersburg PA
CBHW071501040426
42444CB00008B/1445